Principles
of
Markets

Principles of Markets

A.J. Rogers III

THE DRYDEN PRESS INC.
Hinsdale, Illinois

Preface

The series of which this book is a part has been constructed on an assumption that we all hope is correct. The assumption is that undergraduate instruction, and specifically the teaching of economic principles courses is no longer the stepchild of university curricula. There are certainly signs that this assumption is correct. Younger instructors with career commitments to teaching *principles* as well as research and higher level instruction are being put in charge of principles teaching and the structure of the courses. This type of instructor finds the massive classic hardback text less than satisfactory for the needs of today's students. True, many of these paperweights have the advantage that they come in a neat package of instructor's manuals, study guides, test banks, programmed learning work-books, graphics, film strips, etc., until hell won't have it—and neither will the conscientious instructor. The stuff is so pat, so canned, that any inno-vation on his part is lost in the shuffle or breaks the course program in a disruptive way. From the student's standpoint, the multi-revised, "up-to-date" denisons of the academic jungle are a real disaster. Their weight alone is enough to scare the average freshman or sophomore right into the nearest sociology course. When, and if, they actually start to read these jewels, students' original fear turns into sheer panic. I'll wager that there are more used economics principles texts with virtually uncreased spines than any other category of freshman course book.

There is nothing really startling in the series that we have put together. Our purpose has been to give an instructor some choices of material to be presented in the different segments of the principles course. To accomplish this, both the micro and macro portions have been divided somewhat arbitrarily into three segments each. Microeconomics has been split into *trade, markets,* and *microeconomic issues.* Macroeconomics has been divided into sections on *money, aggregates* or *macroeconomic analysis,* and *policy issues.* Within each of these six fields, three short paperback books have been prepared. The three books represent different approaches and different levels of difficulty. As you can see in the outline below, the lowest levels are all entitled "Elements of . . . ," the intermediate levels

MICROECONOMICS			MACROECONOMICS		
Trade	Markets	Issues	Money	Aggregates	Issues
1. Elements of Trade 2. Principles of Trade 3. Theory of Trade	1. Elements of Markets 2. Principles of Markets 3. Theory of Markets	1. Elements of Microeconomic Issues 2. Principles of Microeconomic Issues 3. Theory of Microeconomic Issues	1. Elements of Money 2. Principles of Money 3. Theory of Money	1. Elements of Macroeconomics 2. Principles of Macroeconomics 3. Theory of Macroeconomics	1. Elements of Economic Policy 2. Principles of Economic Policy 3. Theory of Economic Policy

"Principles of . . . ," and finally the highest levels "Theory of . . . ." This use of titles is designed to keep potential confusion between levels at a minimum.

Generally, books in the upper or "Theory" level are heavily analytical in approach and use algebra, geometry, and simple set theory. Books in the intermediate or "Principles" group are aimed at approximately the level of a standard principles text. Simple algebra and geometry are the most sophisticated tools of logic used. The lowest level uses only the very simplest geometry and descriptive material for development of the analysis. None of the books employ much institutional material nor present many straight facts and figures. This we leave to the instructor whose taste for his own materials is likely to be far more effective in teaching than any material we could include.

The whole idea of the series is to give the instructor a chance to *vary* the level of difficulty and method of approach between the several sections. Thus, for example, an instructor might choose the intermediate level for all phases of the course except *money*, where he might wish to use the higher level. We expect a great deal of substitution between the "Elements" and the "Principles" levels. Similarly, we expect a considerable amount of mixing between the "Principles" and "Theory." I doubt if there will be much mixing between the top and bottom levels within the same course although there is certainly nothing to prevent such a mix. Any six books chosen from each of the segments will make a coordinated package covering the complete range of a two semester principles course.

There is a certain amount of overlapping and repetition between the books, and this is intentional. In the first place, it is hoped that many of these books will fulfill the function of supplementing other materials in principles and intermediate courses. But even when used as primarily intended, the overlap provides emphasis and review of the most important concepts developed elsewhere.

In all of the books, there has been an attempt to keep the style as light as possible. Those that think that textbooks should read like journal articles will be very unhappy with this aspect of the series.

One of the key features of this approach is the fact that portions of the series can be quickly and economically revised as the contemporary scene dictates. The system employed by Dryden Press in producing this group of books makes it possible to go from manuscript to finished product in two months. We are living in a revolutionary age when it comes to the passing of information. The authors hope that our approach will take advantage of some of the potential this revolution makes possible. Obviously, your constructive comments will be most welcome. If this product is not exactly what you want, tell us. By maintaining close two-way communication, maybe we can all do a better job of developing a measure of understanding about the world of choices in which all of us, teachers and students, live.

A. J. Rogers, III   Milwaukee, Wisconsin
General Editor   December, 1971

Contents

Contents

Principles
of
Markets

Chapter One   Introduction

You have already learned that for man to rise above a bare subsistence level in his material welfare, some type of specialization in production will be necessary. Specialization, in turn, makes some kind of exchange between men absolutely essential. Very few people will argue with these basic principles. But when it comes to how this exchange is to take place and who is going to benefit by how much, agreement gives way to some of the most violent arguments in history. This book discusses one solution or set of answers to the above questions. We will basically be talking about how the so-called *market system* operates to allocate things that man considers *scarce*.

Any economic system must answer the following problems in one way or another. Given any particular environment with its stock of resources, a decision must be made as to *what* will be produced. This is actually a very complex question including a whole series of sub-questions. For example, are goods that primarily find a use in *consumption* to be produced, or should production be oriented to making things like factories, machine tools, hydroelectric plants, and highways? What breakdown should there be between *consumer goods* and *capital goods*? After that basic decision is made, what specific kinds of things should be produced within each category of resource use? Should we have Cadillacs, Mercedes, Volkswagons, or Vegas? Should we have some of each or all of one kind? Do we have 3-inch thick carpets in the executive suite, or should management personnel operate from quonset huts with pot-bellied stoves to take the chill out of winter weather? At this stage, never mind the potential answers, the point is that the questions exist and must be answered by *any* economic system.

Once the above question set has been disposed of, there still remains the question of *how* all the goods are to be produced. Again, this is a complex question made up of many parts. Should steel, for instance, be produced using a great deal of labor and very little capital? China, not long ago, tried steel production this way. On the other hand, should there be one giant plant producing all the steel requirements of any given economy? Perhaps there should be one country producing all the steel required for the whole world. Crazy? Maybe, but the question is there nonetheless. Also in this broad question arises the problem of what level of use we should make of any natural resource. If we "need" lumber right now, should the redwood forests of the country be stripped, or should the resource use be such as to use only what can be replaced each year or each decade? Should we sacrifice clean streams in northern Wisconsin for cheaper paper products? If so, to what degree? "Clean" is not an absolute term nor is "cheap."

Finally, we come to the question that gets everyone uptight. Once the decisions about what and how are made, *who* is going to get *how much* of the pie? Whatever arguments might arise in answering the first two sets of questions, those arguments will seem puny compared to the hassle over this set of questions. Should people be rewarded according to how much they produce? If so, how do you measure "how much" they produce? By weight? By number of units? By dollar value? Maybe people should be rewarded according to their needs. Fine, but who is going to determine those "needs?" What happens if there simply is not enough around to satisfy all those needs? Somebody is going to have to change their needs or have their needs changed for them.

From all of the above questions, one thing should be obvious; sooner or later some answers must appear probably depending not only on questions of efficiency, or the "best way," but also on what someone or some group of people think is "right," "wrong," "equitable," or "unfair." Sooner or later, some personal value judgments come into the decision-making process. The type of economic system chosen is bound to reflect those value positions to a large degree.

Societies can be organized in three basic ways. Of course, there are many variations on these three themes, but most economic (and political) organizations use one or a combination of these methods. The first can be described as "traditional." In this case, people's actions are primarily governed by the "accepted way of doing things." Governments are often controlled by the sons of sons or "the" families. Codified morals form the basic constraints upon which individual actions are taken. Even in the market place, the notion of a "fair price" often overrides considerations of relative scarcity or abundance. The craft guilds of the middle-ages were classic examples of this system. To the extent that dedication to tradition exceeds dedication to wants, this system can work in terms of answering the basic questions posed above. Dedication can also be assisted by having laws enforced assuring the proper dedication to the "true" values.

The second allocation system consists of a central body of some sort that sits down and *plans* the total operation of the economy. The planning body could be elected or completely totalitarian in its makeup and operation. In essence, individual decision-making is delegated either voluntarily or through coercion to the planning body, whose responsibility it is to answer the economic questions. Their answers may be implemented in a variety of ways including use of the market system—the subject of this book. The assumption underlying this kind of organization is that for some reason or other, the ruling or controlling group knows what is best for the individual better than the individual does himself. Either this assumption has to be made, or the following assumption: Individual action imposes costs on other individuals making the group "worse off."

An underlying assumption of the market system we will be discussing, is that individual freedom of choice should be as great as possible, so long as such choices do not impose unreimbursed costs on others. Note, however, that the free-choice assumption remains. Some people would argue that the market system (in pure form) is the one system not depending on value judgments. This is nonsense. The value position of individual freedom may be more popular than some others, but it remains a value position nevertheless.

During the discussions that follow, several points are to be kept in mind. First, much of the presentation will be in terms of theoretically perfect conditions. Do not get the idea that just because the real world is not perfect, the arguments are invalid. The models give us benchmarks by which actual events can be compared. This is useful so long as the assumptions are remembered and the results tempered accordingly. Second, while the solutions to economic questions will be couched in terms of the market system, do not forget that these *questions* must be answered in any economy. In other words, whether a market exists or not, market *functions* must be carried out in any economy.

Organizationally, the next chapter will present an overview of market operations. The two chapters that follow will examine in much more detail the concepts of supply and demand, and what determines their size. A discussion of the various implications contained in this book is presented in the next volume of this series dealing with microeconomic issues.

Chapter Two

An Overview of the Market

What is a market? *Webster's Collegiate Dictionary* has several definitions, most of which referring to a geographic area in which buyers and sellers come together. One definition, however, seems to hit the modern day usage a bit better. It states, ". . . the course of commercial activity by which the exchange of commodities is effected . . ." The time was when a geographic spot was essential for a market activity. However, with today's communications facilities, market activities can take place with the physical separation of buyers and sellers over half the globe.

While the methods of the market have changed, its purpose in the scheme of things remains unchanged since the dawn of time. Basically, someone has something, item A, that is scarce. Someone else has a desire for that scarce item A. Person II gives up another scarce item B to person I in exchange for item A. This simple act can get quite complicated as many commodities and many people get into the act. But the magnificent simplicity should never be forgotten. Individuals engage in trade because the exchange process allows them to increase their wellbeing. The market allows people to use goods which they value relatively less to purchase other goods of greater relative value.

Exchange is one of the two ways in which man can increase his material wellbeing. The other, of course, is the process of production. Production takes one set of goods as inputs and transforms these goods into something else of greater value to someone. Exchange does not transform the goods. But exchange makes it possible to increase human utility, or satisfaction, by allowing people to obtain the items most valuable *to them*. As pointed out many times before, trade and exchange also makes the whole business of specialization in production feasible. Without it, each and every person would have to perform all of the productive functions for wanted goods by themselves.

Using a Venn diagram, this can be easily illustrated. In Figure 2.1, the universe of wanted but scarce goods is represented. What man tries to do is expand the center subset of attainable goods to minimize *scarcity* as he knows it. He tries to make the band outside of the attainable goods but inside the universe of wanted goods as small as possible. One way to do this is to expand the production of scarce goods. The other way is to gain more satisfaction, increase utility, out of the available goods by obtaining that *bundle* which is most desired. Productive activities attempt the first action while exchange attempts the second. Exchange makes it possible to obtain the most desired goods, and by permitting specialization, it also can increase the production of scarce goods. Of course, another way of reducing scarcity is to reduce people's desires for goods. Sometimes this can be accomplished by dedication to something such as "the community," "the revolution," "the family," etc.

We also illustrate the impact of production and trade by using the tools developed in the volume on trade. Consider, for example, a utility function representing the combined utilities of everyone in a given community. This aggregation has many problems, both conceptually and empirically, but for this particular purpose, the problems would not change the nature of our analytical results. In Figure 2.2, a set of community indifference

Figure 2.1
Production, Exchange and Scarcity

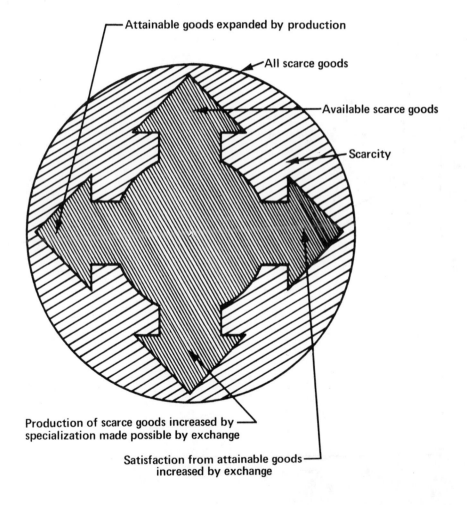

Figure 2.2
Gain from Trade

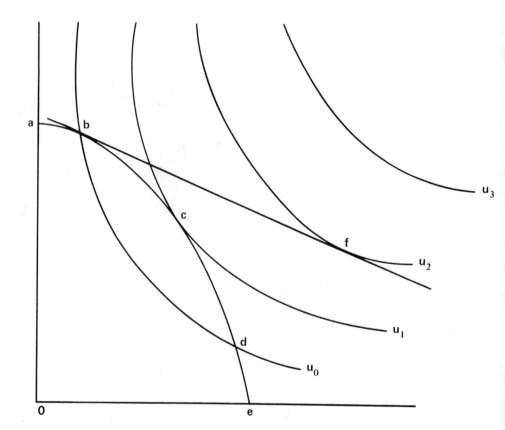

curves has been constructed $(u_0, u_1, u_2,$ and $u_3)$. In addition, we will simplify the world into two goods: A and B. If you wish, consider one of the goods as something specific, and the other single good as the bundle of everything else produced. We have shown the production possibilities as having increasing costs. As specialization in one good is approached, the costs of producing it in terms of the foregone other good goes up. This characteristic is generally found in the world, although it is not needed for this particular analysis.

Let's consider the impact first of *domestic* trade, that is, trade within the economy itself. Without such trade, production could be taking place at any point on the production possibilities curve *abcde*. There is no assurance whatsoever that such a production point would maximize the utility or welfare of the community. Even though all resources were being efficie.tly employed, production taking place on the production possibilities curve itself, such a point could be *b* or *d* as well as *c*. At point *c*, community welfare is maximized—the highest possible indifference curve is reached. But without trade, there would be no way of determining this fact. Only the operation of the market can bring about the optimum production combination represented by point *c*.

Of course, expanding the argument to include trade outside the economy, specialization can permit production of goods in which the economy has a comparative advantage, and in which foreign trade permits consumption beyond the production constraint of the domestic economy itself. In Figure 2.2, such a point is shown at *f*. If this seems unclear or unfamiliar, you should go back and review the trade section of a good principles text.

Gains from economic growth or development are illustrated in Figure 2.3. In this instance, community utility is increased because the production possibilities of the community have been increased. The boundary of attainable production points has moved from *abc* to *def*. The utility derived by the community has gone up from u_0 to u_1.

For both gains from production and gains from exchange to take place, some kind of market function—some means of exchange—must exist. It can be fulfilled by plan, that is, by order of some directing body; or it can be accomplished by an actual market operation involving the interaction of buyers and sellers. Of course, it can also be a combination of these two extremes. A market may exist in which certain boundaries or constraints are placed on the actions of individual buyers and sellers, but then the market is allowed to operate within those constraints. Prescription drugs,

Figure 2.3
Gains from Development

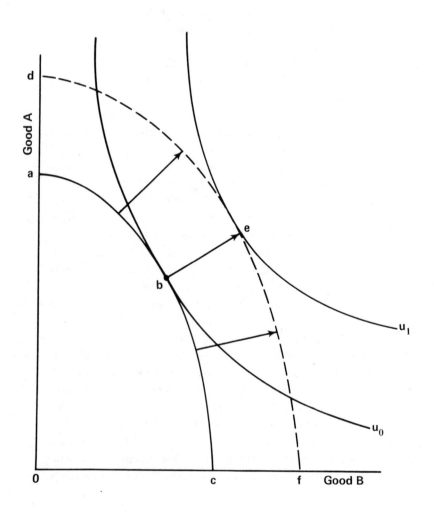

for instance, are banned from general sale to the public at large. Instead, authority to purchase is required from a medical practitioner. Once this authority is obtained, however, the market will determine the price. In this case, the market is probably *very* imperfect, but nevertheless it is operating. More on this type of market will be covered in the next volume.

One more point must be discussed before getting to the specifics of supply and demand: Have you ever really sat down and figured out just what the market buys and sells? Probably not, but the question is both interesting and important. It really boils down to the question of why one buys anything. Goods are wanted because of what they can do for us. They are wanted for the services they can perform. There is no circumstance in which anyone wants something "for itself." *Always*, there is some flow of services from the good that provides its holder with utility. These services may be unusual in the everyday sense. For example, the owner of a fine work of art may derive pleasure from being able to look at the painting or sculpture whenever he pleases. This is clearly a service. He may also derive utility from the fact of ownership. You might say that this is owning something "for itself," but I would argue, and in fact define, this phenomenon as a flow of services. It may be a keeping-up-with-the-Jones' service or a snob service, but a service it is nevertheless.

Given that things are puchased to obtain the services of the item concerned, what then is really purchased? The answer is that a certain bundle of *property rights* over a good are obtained when the good is purchased. You are buying the rights to use some good in specific ways. It is rare indeed, however, when that bundle of ownership rights is completely without restriction. When you buy an automobile, for instance, you buy the right to use it in certain prescribed ways and in certain prescribed places. You buy the right to destroy it, if you wish, as long as such destruction does not impose costs on others. You also buy the right to transfer the car to someone else should you so desire. Finally, you buy the right to prohibit others from using your car if you do not want them to. These are the basic rights one purchases when ownership is gained in *fee simple*. They include the rights to use, transfer, destroy, and limit use. Note, however, that you are not allowed to use your car for the purpose of killing other people. You may do so, but the law will take a very dim view of this and probably impose substantial costs on you for such an action. You will also be chastised if you drive your vehicle across the lawns in the city park, or exceed limits on use such as speed, parking, or stopping at red traffic lights. The point is that *ownership* of anything is not a simple nor absolute concept. All that you own and all that you buy in the marketplace is a series of use-rights that vary with the good and society's feelings about the use of that good.

Of course, there are also markets for the services of goods that include getting some rights, but fewer than the fee simple bundle. Leasing arrangements of various sorts provide examples of this sort of purchase. If you lease an automobile, you can still use it in virtually the same ways that you could use a purchased car. However, you cannot transfer the car to someone else. You don't *own* it. You cannot destroy it without further cost. Again, you don't *own* it. You can limit other people's use of the car in much the same way that ownership would permit.

As we will see later on, there are some economic facts of life that govern the type of property rights people try to obtain over goods and services. But in the meantime, it is important that you realize just what we are going to be talking about for the rest of this book: We will be talking about changes in the holding of property rights over things which yield services. This is what the market is all about.

Chapter Three

Demand

The whole discussion of the market and its operation will revolve around the interaction of elements that make people want goods and elements that make people willing and able to produce goods. In other words, we will be talking about the demand for goods and the supply of goods.

We have already talked in a very general way about the reasons why anyone wants and is willing to pay for anything. The simplistic answer was merely to get the *services* which a good can provide. Now it's time to consider a more detailed breakdown of the factors that influence the quantity of any good people will be willing and able to purchase. We're going to use implicit function notation, but don't let that worry you. It's strictly shorthand and nothing more.

The quantity demanded of any good will depend upon the price of the good itself, the price of other goods that are related to the use of the given good, the incomes of demanders, the tastes of demanders, and the market transactions costs associated with the demander's purchase. In symbols,

$$q_d = f(p, p_r, i, t, ICP_c)$$

where:

q_d = quantity demanded of the given good.

p = price of the given good.

p_r = prices of related goods, complements or substitutes.

i = incomes of demanders.

t = tastes of demanders.

ICP_d = transactions costs (information, contractual, and policing costs).

Let's look at each of these variables separately as far as they influence quantity demanded. First, we have the price of the good itself. Remember what we mean by price: The price of a good is the *per unit cost* of that good. It is whatever must be given up per unit of the thing acquired. Very often this is expressed in money terms, but there is absolutely no reason why this couldn't be expressed just as well in boxtops, jellybeans, or anything else that had a mutual value to the buyer and seller. While you probably don't think of it this way very often, the *price* of a good also represents the *opportunity cost* of purchasing the good. It represents the value of something else that is given up or something else that now cannot be purchased with the same resources. You should have already learned that opportunity costs are probably the most important and yet most ignored phenomenon in economics.

We are particularly interested in the price of a good and its influence on both supply and demand. Given a market system, it is the price of the good which is expected to bring about an equilibrium situation—a situation in which there are no forces tending to change the quantities supplied and demanded. As we proceed, you will note that the price of the good is the only argument (variable) included in both the demand function and the supply function.

Depending upon what you are holding constant, either the quantity demanded of a good *always* varies inversely as its price or the quantity of a good demanded *almost always* varies inversely as its price. If one conceptually holds everything constant, including real income, then the *Law of*

Demand states that price rises will always cause a decrease in the quantity of a good demanded. There are limiting cases where demand is perfectly elastic or perfectly inelastic, which will be explained later. There will never be a situation, however, in which a fall in price will cause a decrease in quantity demanded, or a raise in price that will cause an increase in quantity demanded, *ceteris paribus* (everything else being equal).

We will be deriving the relationship between price and quantity demanded just as soon as the influence of the rest of the arguments in the demand function are given some initial consideration. But right now you should know that the relationship between price and quantity demanded is so important that the relationship itself is called the *demand* for a commodity. ***Demand is not the same thing as quantity demanded.*** Demand is the whole series of different prices and the quantities demanded at each of those prices. Figure 3.1 graphs a *demand curve* showing this inverse relationship between price and quantity demanded, *ceteris paribus*. Bars over the arguments indicate this constant condition.

The second argument in the demand function consists of the prices of related goods. This variable is actually a series of variables. The price of any good whose consumption is related in some way to the consumption of the given good will affect the quantity demanded of the given good. There are two categories which produce opposite results on quantity demanded. First, some goods have substitutes. You all know generally what this means. If some people are willing to substitute some of the services of one good for another, then some degree of substitution exists. The old chestnuts of butter and margarine are often cited as examples of substitute goods. Volkswagons and Pintos are substitutes for some people under some circumstances. I'm sure you can see that the price of a substitute is very liable to have an influence on the quantity demanded of the given good. If the price of Volkswagons goes up, for instance, this will make owning a VW more expensive relative to the cost of owning a Pinto. Therefore it would be reasonable to expect that the quantity of Pintos demanded at any given price would rise.

It is precisely the above mentioned hope that led President Nixon to impose a surcharge on imports late in the summer of 1971. The idea was to stimulate the demand for American-made products which had been facing increased competition from foreign imports. By imposing an import surcharge, the price of VW's and other foreign-made autos rose. To the degree that substitution did exist between the foreign and domestic autos,

Figure 3.1
A Demand Curve

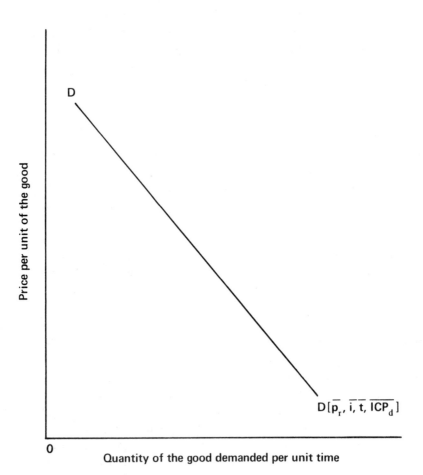

D

$D[\overline{p_r},\ \overline{i},\ \overline{t},\ \overline{ICP_d}]$

Price per unit of the good

0

Quantity of the good demanded per unit time

Figure 3.2
A Change in the Demand for Domestic Automobiles

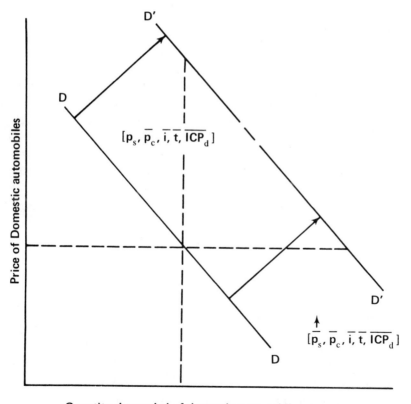

Quantity demanded of domestic automobiles per year

demand for the domestic product would rise. At any given price for the domestic product, the quantity demanded would be greater. This is what is meant by an *increase in demand*. The whole schedule of prices and quantities demanded shift upward. In Figure 3.2, such a shift in demand is illustrated. Schedule *DD* shows demand with all other arguments in the demand function being held constant. Notice again the notation using bars on top of the variables to denote their constant state. Schedule *D'D'* shows *demand* for domestic autos after the *price* of foreign autos had been increased. Here note the notation which shows the price of a substitute having been raised.

The other kind of related good is called a *complement*. Any good which is used together with another good is likely to be complementary. Most automobiles require four tires for each car. Sometimes a fifth is kept for a spare. But if your auto does not have at least four tires, the chances are the local police will be slightly unhappy at the racket the bare wheels will make. Your ride will be something less than perfectly comfortable, too. But with four tires, the car can ride like a dream and be as quiet as last year's politician. Obviously, when complementary goods are being used, the prime concern of the consumer is the total cost of using the package. Therefore, if the price of one item in the package goes up, the cost of consuming the package goes up too. From this it follows that an increase in the price of a complementary good will *decrease* the quantity demanded of the given good. If the price of automobiles goes up, then, *ceteris paribus*, the quantity demanded of tires will probably fall. The reverse relationship is probably less sensitive, but nevertheless, it would exist as well. If the price of tires increased sufficiently, the demand for automobiles could be expected to go down, probably not much, but down at least a little.

Figure 3.3 illustrates a decrease in demand brought about by an increase in the price of a complementary good. The original demand relationship, *DD*, is drawn with the usual *ceteris paribus* assumption. Everything else, including prices of all related goods, is held constant. Next we allow the price of automobiles to rise. Now, for each price and quantity demanded for tires, the cost of consuming the auto/tires package has risen. Therefore, the quantity demanded of tires will fall for each price. The demand curve shifts downward to the left to *D'D'*. Note, there are two ways this change can be viewed. First, at any given price of tires, the quantity demanded will be smaller. However, it is also true that for any

Figure 3.3
A Change in the Demand for Automobile Tires

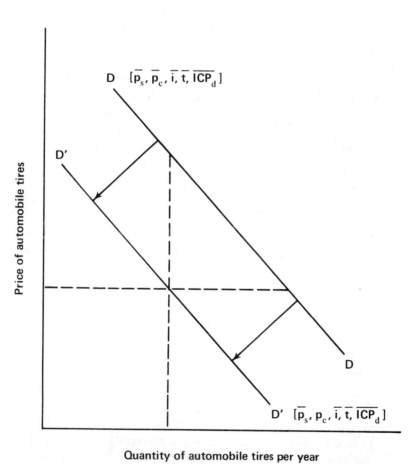

Quantity of automobile tires per year

given quantity demanded, the price will have to be lower. The shift in demand implies both of these changes.

In the case of both substitutes and complements, we actually define their status by describing the price change/demand change relationship. If a change in the price of one good changes demand for a second good in the *same* direction, then the goods are defined as substitutes. If a change in the price of one good produces an *opposite* change in the demand for another good, the two are defined as complements. The degree of the relative changes is described by what is called the *cross elasticity of demand* which will be described a bit later in the book.

The next argument in our demand function to be discussed is the income of the demanders of the product. You probably think this is a simple one. As incomes go up, the quantity demanded of any good is going to go up, and vice versa, right? Maybe. For many goods, this is precisely what happens. As the income, and hence the buying power, of demanders goes up their willingness and ability to purchase many items increases. Certainly this is true for something like sirloin steak. But is it true as well for navy beans? The answer is no. Some goods that are often associated with low budgets are known as *inferior goods*. For them, an increase in the income of potential buyers means a decrease in the quantity demanded at any given price. In other words, for inferior goods, an increase in incomes means a decrease in demand. Conversely, for *normal* or *superior goods*, an increase in the incomes of demanders will result in an increase in the demand for the product. Some goods might be normal at one stage of income development, but become inferior as incomes continued to rise. Rice in a country like India would probably exhibit such a dual characteristic. As the almost sub-subsistence incomes of people increased somewhat, their demand for the staple in their diet would get larger. However, were the incomes of the people to continue their rise, other things would probably take over as wants and needs after the basic rice requirement had been met.

As a matter of fact, the general category of food probably exhibits this income-demand relationship as illustrated in Figure 3.4. At low levels of income, income increases result in larger quantities of food demanded. Beyond certain income levels, however, further income increases are spent on other things beside food. Some of those other things might be related to food purchases such as packaging or pre-prepared food products, etc. In this case, the expenditure on food and related products would increase,

Figure 3.4
Income and Demand

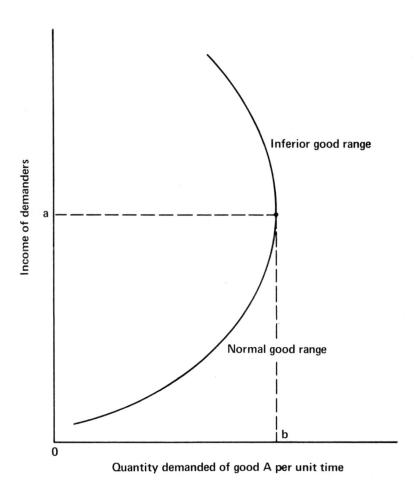

while the amount being paid for the actual food itself was decreasing. Figure 3.4 shows an income-quantity demanded graph of such an item. Below income level *Oa*, increases in incomes cause increases in the quantity demanded of the good. At income levels greater than *Oa*, the purchases of the good fall with further income increases. The good begins as a normal good but becomes inferior as the prosperity of its buyers increases.

As you will see, this relationship can be defined precisely using what is called the *income elasticity of demand*. When changes in income produce opposite changes in quantity demanded, the good is inferior, and when the changes are in the same direction, the good is normal or superior.

The next category of variables which affect the quantity demanded of any good is something called *tastes*. Tastes are those quirks of human nature that really include all of the psychic factors not covered explicitly by the other arguments in the demand function. It may be something as earthshaking as the style of the mini-skirt, or as frivolous as the frisbee being tossed around on the beach. We leave the "whys" of tastes and style to the designers and the psychologists. The impact of tastes, however, is clearly in our arena as economists. The impact on demand itself, of a change in tastes, is obvious. If tastes "increase" in some sense of the word, then the quantity buyers will demand at any given price will increase, or the price they are willing and able to pay for any given quantity will be larger.

The final argument in our demand function is the item of *transactions costs*. We will be talking a great deal about the "free" market, that is, the market uninhibited by outside constraints. That's fair enough, but in another sense the market is anything but free. The operation of the market system requires the expenditure of resources just as surely as the operation of any productive plant. These costs of operation will impinge on both the supply of the product and the demand for that product. We have divided transactions costs into three categories: (1) Information costs, (2) Contractual costs, and (3) Policing costs. (ICP—costs.) Let's take a look at each of these three variables.

Any rational action anyone takes requires information about the potential costs and benefits of such action. The better the available information, the greater the probability that that act will result in a net benefit to the actor. For the market system to produce anything that even approaches optimum welfare, good information must be available to both buyers and sellers. But information is not a free good. Virtually all useful information is obtained only at a cost to someone. Sometimes a great deal of not very useful information is created at considerable cost, too. Certain TV ads could be cited as examples. But without some kind of information about alternatives and their costs, the market in anything would cease to operate. All of the everyday purchases you make are based on at least some information. Very often, this information is paid for by the supplier rather than as a direct charge to you. You will still bear a portion of the expense through the purchase price of the product concerned, but the initial shot will affect the supplier's costs. Such is not always the case, however. If you buy a newspaper to look at the classified ads, you are purchasing market information. When you take half a day and do some comparison shopping, you are paying a substantial sum in foregone use of time to get market information. Even if you adopt the attitude that you cannot afford to waste time comparison shopping, and take the first deal that comes along, you will be paying an information cost. In this case, the cost will be the higher product price as compared to the deal you could have gotten by shopping around. For most individuals, information costs consist primarily of time expenditures. For firms who are demanders of factors of production, however, information costs can become a major item. The company that spends thousands of dollars maintaining an employment office is spending resources on information. Of course, firms spend tremendous quantities of funds on market research, but this falls in the other category of suppliers' ICP costs which will be considered later.

How about the second group of transactions costs? Every sale or purchase involves the transfer of certain property rights from one person or entity to another. Such a sale is, in fact, a contract. The law will be glad to enforce the terms of any legitimately made sale. Again, most of the minor purchases made by most individuals do not involve any large or obvious amount of contractual costs. Yet every purchase involves at least some contract expense. When checking out at the local supermarket you generally have to wait in line. Here again, time is not a free good. Of course, on major purchases such as real estate, the contractual expenses can get to be a big item. Lawyers' fees, recording fees, closing costs of one type or another—all these are contractual costs that impinge directly on the demander of the product.

Finally, there is the category of policing costs. Many will probably wonder how policing costs get into the act as a transactions cost. A brief excursion into an example should illustrate the point. Most of you live somewhere. Some of you, or your parents, probably own your dwelling. Others of you rent quarters. For at least a portion of you, housing is a free good. You are not required to give up anything to get it. But somebody is giving up resources for the housing you are occupying because housing in general is *not* a free good. From our discussions before, remember that with either owning or renting, what is actually involved is control over certain bundles of property rights. The rights will vary with the type of ownership or rental arrangement. But, in essence, they will provide you with the service of *housing*. Other services such as prestige factors or investment protection may also be part of the package. But basic housing is at least one of the services derived from having property rights over your quarters.

Now imagine that tomorrow morning congress passes a brand new law eliminating all property rights in connection with housing. The government is not going to confiscate the property, they just are not going to enforce any contract or agreement involving housing property. If you owned a house before, you don't own it any more. If you were renting, you no longer have an enforceable lease. Of course, this cuts two ways. Your landlord cannot collect any rent from you, but there is nothing to give you any particular right to live there either. Some guy comes in off the street and announces that he is going to live there from now on. You call the cops but find that there isn't one thing they can or will do about it. With the destruction of specific rights, the rights have become general and the guy off the street has just as much "right" to be in your house as you do. It doesn't take much of an imagination to figure out the chaos that would soon result. For one thing, nobody would take care of housing anymore. There would be no assurance that maintenance efforts would benefit the person making the effort. The production of new housing would come to a screeching halt. Nobody in their right mind would "buy" housing. There is nothing left to buy. Rights have become general, and any specific rights are no longer enforceable. You could hire your own private army to protect what used to be your rights, but the problem here is that any kind of action against an attempted interloper would be illegal.

From this extreme example, one can see just what policing has to do with the market. Rights are the only thing that are traded, and rights are meaningless unless they can be enforced. Do not make the mistake of thinking that all we are talking about are *private* property rights; we are talking about all rights, whether they are held privately or by some collec-

Figure 3.5
Demand Variables

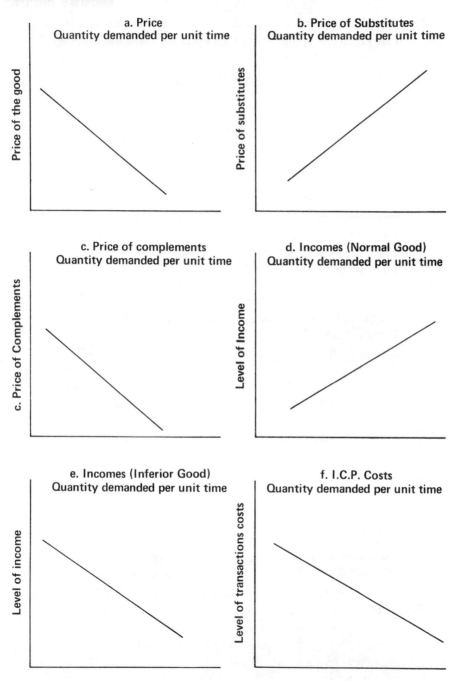

a. Price
Quantity demanded per unit time

b. Price of Substitutes
Quantity demanded per unit time

c. Price of complements
Quantity demanded per unit time

d. Incomes (Normal Good)
Quantity demanded per unit time

e. Incomes (Inferior Good)
Quantity demanded per unit time

f. I.C.P. Costs
Quantity demanded per unit time

tive group. Without enforcement of some kind, a right becomes meaningless. The more it costs to enforce rights, the more expensive will be the total package of deriving services from purchased goods. As an example, as violence increases in inner-city areas, many shopkeepers institute their own protective systems. These may consist of special burglar alarms, police dogs, private police, etc. As a result of the increased cost of policing the rights they supposedly have over their property, the demand for the property itself decreases. And so it is. An increase in any of the transactions costs impinging on demanders will tend to reduce the demand for the good in question.

Well, there you have it. We've covered all of the variables which can affect the quantity of any marketed good demanded. The graphs in Figure 3.5 recap the influence of each of the arguments in the demand function. In each case, the quantity demanded per unit time is plotted on the horizontal axis, and the variable in question is plotted on the vertical axis. Thus, in Figure 3.5a, the familiar demand curve shows the *ceteris paribus* relationship between the price of a good and the quantity demanded of that good. The curve is downward sloping to the right showing the *Law of Demand*. Figure 3.5b shows the relationship between the price of a substitute good and the quantity demanded of a given good. As the price of a substitute increases, the demand for the given good increases as well. The opposite is true for complementary goods as shown in Figure 3.5c. As the price of a complement increases, the demand for the given good decreases. The effect of income on the demand for a normal good is illustrated in Figure 3.5d (direct) and that for an inferior good is illustrated in Figure 3.5e (inverse). Finally, in Figure 3.5f, the effects of transactions costs on demand is shown. No graph is given for increasing tastes since putting a numerical value on changes in taste is difficult if not impossible.

Derivation of Demand

It is obvious that the demand for a good will depend upon the utility function of the demander or demanders. By going back to the utility function and the assumptions that are made in that analysis, a great deal of insight can be obtained into the operation of the demand portion of the market.

When the utility function was first constructed in this series, back in the volume on trade, several assumptions were implied, although not specifically stated, at the time. These were:

1. People prefer more to less. Satiety is possible for a single good, but not possible for all economic goods at the same time.

2. People can and do *order* their preferences. They can determine *for themselves* which attainable bundle of goods is preferable to any alternative bundle or is equally prefered to an alternative bundle.

3. If one bundle of goods is preferred to a second, and the second is preferred to a third, then the first is also preferred to the third. This is the axiom of *transitivity* that merely states that people are consistent in their preferences.

4. If the quantity of one good is reduced, the amount that must be added of a second good to maintain the same level of satisfaction must be increased. This is the old business of the decreasing marginal rate of substitution (MRS).

Given these fairly simple and realistic propositions, a utility function can be illustrated using indifference curves such as the one in Figure 3.6. The non-satiety proposition is shown by the continuous increase in utility as more of both goods are acquired. The ordering axiom assures that we can in fact construct a utility surface with the *comparative* utility of different bundles identified. The transitivity axiom assures that no two indifference curves will ever touch or cross. There is one and only one level of utility associated with each and every possible bundle of goods. Finally, the decreasing MRS proposition is illustrated by the fact that the indifference curves are convex to the origin of the graph.

On the vertical axis, we will plot the *dollar value* of all commodities except good X. On the horizontal axis we will plot the *quantity* of good X. The utility map, therefore, shows the trade-off between quantities of good X and all other goods except X. Three indifference curves are drawn in the diagram, u_0, u_1, and u_2, representing increasing levels of utility. Next, a *budget constraint* is imposed. If, on the one hand, all of this person's resources were taken in goods other than X, the value of that bundle would be $100. At the highest price of X (budget constraint line x_1), were he to take all of his resources in good X, he could hold 10 units. As the price of X gets cheaper, he could use all of his resources and get more X. Were the budget constraint line equal to x_2, he could get 20 units of X. A budget constraint equal to x_3 would allow him to hold 30 units of X as long as he held nothing else.

The question, of course, is how much X and how much of the alternative to X will he actually hold. To determine this we find the highest indifference curve that can be reached with each given budget line. In the

Figure 3.6
Deriving Price and Quantity Demanded

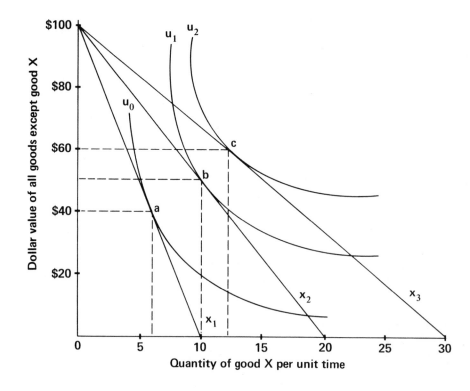

case of budget line x_1, the highest indifference curve that can be reached is u_0. At point a, u_0 is tangent to x_1. Point a represents the combination of $40 worth of other goods and 6 units of good X. When the price of X is lowered to budget line x_2, indifference curve u_1 can be reached, which represents $50 worth of non-X goods and 10 units of X. (Don't confuse the fact that budget line x_1 hits the horizontal axis at 10 units and point b represents holding 10 units. This is coincidence and has no significance.) Lowering the price of X still further to budget line x_3 will mean a still higher indifference curve with the new bundle consisting now of 12 units of X and $60 dollars worth of other goods. We now have a series of three prices and their corresponding quantities demanded.

In Figure 3.7, these points are plotted in the form of a demand curve for good X. It is just what we would have expected in terms of its general slope—downward to the right. As the price of X decreases, the quantity demanded of X increases. Everything else being equal, there's the old *Law of Demand*. But in this case, everything else is not quite equal. As the budget constraint line rotates outward, making the price of X cheaper in terms of all other alternative goods, this reduction in the price of X also increases the effective buying power of the $100. The area of the graph leftward from the budget constraint has gotten larger. Real income has increased. This makes perfectly good sense; if the price of something you have been buying decreases, then you could buy the same quantity as before and have money left over. The fact that the price of one of the goods in your "market basket" has gone down means your command over other goods has gone up. Your real income has increased. This result of a price change on the buying power of the demanders of the good is called the *income effect*. In the paragraphs that follow we will see how this income effect along with something called the *substitution effect* works together or at odds in changing the quantity demanded of a good when the price of the good changes.

In Figure 3.8, we have reconstucted the first change in price of good X from the previous example. The initial budget line was *jf* with *Od* of X held and *ad* of all other goods. A change in the price of X rotated the budget constraint out to *jh* allowing a higher level of utility to be reached, u_1. The total increase in the holding of good X amounts to *df*. In other words, the movement from point a on the initial indifference curve to point b on the higher indifference curve resulted in changing the quantity demanded of X from *Od* to *Of*. Part of this increase in quantity demanded was the result of higher real income caused by the reduced price of X. The other part of the

Figure 3.7
The Demand for Good X

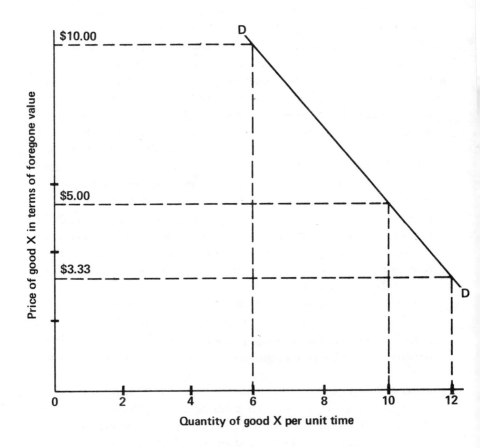

Figure 3.8
Income and Substitution Effects

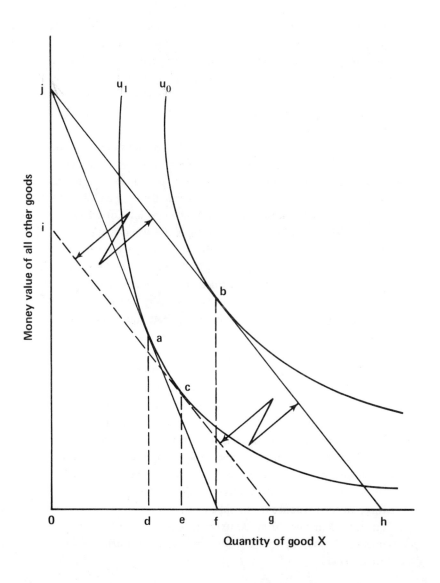

increase is attributable to the fact that X is now cheaper vis-a-vis all other goods than it was before. As a result, more of X is consumed in comparison to all other goods. The price decrease in X has resulted in X being *substituted* for the now more expensive alternatives. This substitution effect *always* works in an inverse direction to the price change. The effect of substitution is always negative with respect to the price change.

Conceptually, isolating the two different effects is simple enough. In practice, it is a different story. What we would like to know is how much more X would have been consumed as the result of *just* the change in relative prices (X compared to all other goods). What this really asks is what quantity of X *at the new price level* would yield exactly the same level of utility as existed before the price change. To answer this question, we must take away income until we arrive back at the original level of utility, u_0.

Graphically, this is simple enough. The new set of relative prices is given by the slope of the new budget constraint *jh*. All we have to do is slide the new budget constraint back until it is just tangent to the old level of utility. On the graph, *ig* is constructed parallel to *jh* and just tangent to u_0 at point *c*. That's all there is to it. At the new level of prices, *0e* of good X would yield the same utility as *0d* of X did when X was more expensive. The straight substitution caused by the price change amounts to an increase in the quantity demanded of X equal to *de*. Of course, the actual increase in the quantity demanded of X amounts to *df*. The difference between *de* and *df* is the amount that quantity demanded increased due to the income effect. The sum of the two effects equals the total change.

In this particular example, the income effect was also negative. This does not have to be the case, however. If the good under consideration is inferior, then increases in income would cause decreases in the quantity demanded. Thus, in our present example, the price of the good falls. This means real income tends upward. The upward movement of income results in a decrease in the quantity demanded. Mind you, the substitution effect is still going on and is still negative. In this case, then, income effect and substitution effect will be operating in opposite directions. Figure 3.9 illustrates the point. In this case, the utility function is such that a change (decrease) in price still results in more of the good being demanded because of the existence of the substitution effect. By itself this increases the quantity demanded from *0d* to *0e*. However, the income effect in this case operates in the opposite direction, reducing the impact of the substitution effect by *ef*.

Figure 3.9
Income Effect with an Inferior Good

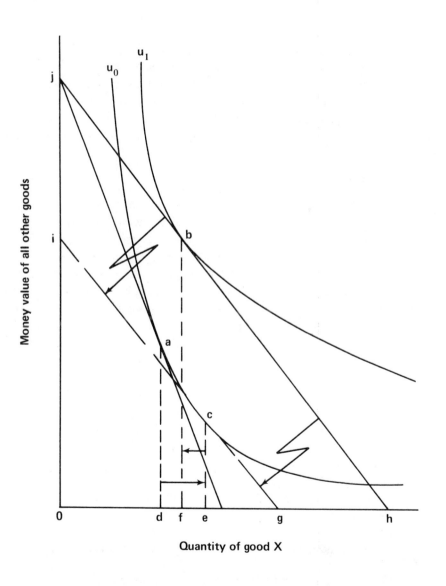

Quantity of good X

It has been suggested that there might be goods so strongly inferior that a decrease in their price might actually decrease the quantity demanded of the good. This would produce what is known as a *Giffen Good*. Such a situation would refute the *Law of Demand*. There has never been a documented case of a Giffen Good so it remains little more than a theoretical possibility.

As you can easily see, the importance of the income effect is going to be very little on most of the day to day purchases we make. If the price of a box of salt doubles, the reduction in purchasing power that results is not going to affect our spending habits very much. However, if the price of housing in one form or another goes up by 10 or 15 percent, we'll all feel the pinch. Clearly, the income effect will be significant *to the individual* only on purchases that represent a fairly large portion of his total budget. When we get to the discussion of elasticity, this point will be reenforced.

Consumers' Surplus

How many "bargains" are you able to pick up during the course of a normal week? Most people would answer this question in terms of the pair of shoes that was marked down 20 percent or the sale on ground beef at the supermarket. But let's define bargain as any price that you actually pay which is less than the absolute maximum you would have been willing to pay on an all-or-nothing basis. The chances are that for most items you buy, if the price went up just a little, you would still buy the item. True, there are some items for which even one lousy cent of price increase would turn off your purchases. There are other items which, given a small price decrease, would become part of your market basket.

All we are really describing here is the downward slope of any demand curve. We are again saying that as the price of a good decreases, the quantity demanded of that good will increase. If we take your own demand plus the demand of others for the same item, this is the pattern that is bound to develop, everything else being held constant. What this means, then, is that at any given price below the maximum on the demand curve, there are some people that would have been willing and able to pay a higher price than the one they are actually paying. A look at Figure 3.10 will help illustrate the point.

According to the demand curve as constructed in the diagram, there is at least one person in the city of Milwaukee willing to pay a price of *Og* for

Figure 3.10
Demand and Consumer Surplus

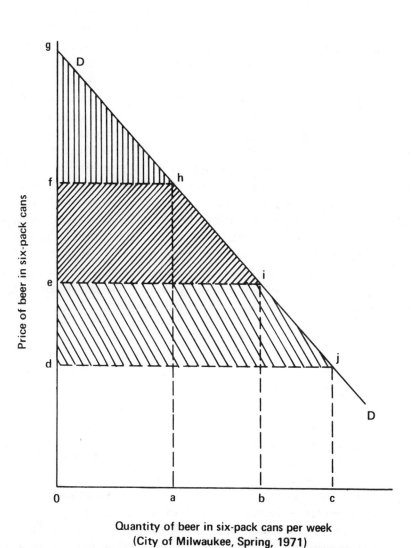

Quantity of beer in six-pack cans per week
(City of Milwaukee, Spring, 1971)

a small quantity of the city's finest product. If the price goes above *Og*, no one will buy any beer whatsoever. As the price falls from *Og*, more and more people will be willing and able to buy more and more beer. At price *Of*, quantity *Oa* will be demanded. But notice, if you had been able to go to each person who wanted beer in the quantity range *Oa*, and if you had been able to extract the last penny from each of them—the absolute maximum each would have paid—you could have collected additional monies in the amount equal to the area of triangle *fhg*. With a single market price of *Of*, the total monies paid out for that quantity of beer equals the area of rectangle *Oahf*. If all possible monies had been extracted from the buyers, the total would have equalled *Oahg*. The difference between what consumers actually pay with a single market price and the amount they would have been willing and able to pay on an all or nothing basis is called *consumers surplus*. Note that as the price of the product gets lower, the amount of the consumers' surplus increases. Thus, at a single price *Oe*, the consumers' surplus increases to *eig*. At the lower market price *Od*, consumers' surplus has risen to *djg*. This merely confirms the obvious; as the price of a good falls, those who buy the good become better off. Lowering the price of a product increases the breadth of the market for the good. In addition, those who would have been willing to purchase the good at higher prices get a better "bargain" than before.

As you will see, the concept of consumer surplus is useful in analyzing the welfare effects of both a freely operating market as well as markets in which controls of one sort or another are imposed.

Elasticity

Thus far we have made some general observations about the behavior of demand. We have discussed the *direction* one variable can be expected to move given a change in another variable. Obviously, the degree of expected movement is also an item of considerable interest, and that's what elasticity is all about. We will begin this discussion by talking about the price elasticity of demand, but the discussion will be generalized later to include the relative movement of any two variables.

The basic question we want to answer is, "How does one go about measuring the degree of change between two interdependent variables?" I say that quantity demanded goes down when the price of a good goes up. Fair enough, but the degree of change is often just as important as the direction. If I were your friendly grocer operating a rip-off store in the inner city, I already know that lowering the price on most items in my store will result in selling more of the items. But I want to know *how much more*. Would it be enough to bring the total volume of sales above the previous level? Would my profit increase or decrease as the result of such a price lowering?

Some of you may think that the answer to this problem is ridiculously simple. All you have to do is describe how many units quantity demanded goes up for every dollar the price falls. This can be done all right, but it really won't help much, because a one dollar price change when you're talking about a $100 item will *not* be the same sort of thing as a one dollar price change on a $2 item. In the first instance, price changed by one percent and in the latter by 50 percent. The same sort of thing holds for changes in quantity. A one unit change in 1,000 units is a very different phenomenon than a one unit change in 10 units.

I'm sure you can easily see what's coming next. To talk meaningfully about changes in either prices or quantities, it is necessary to talk about proportional changes, or percentage changes if you prefer. Once changes are discussed in these terms, some interesting and useful results occur. Perhaps the best way to show this is to go through the mechanics first, and then see what it all means. So, first of all, we will define elasticity as the rate of change in one variable induced by a change in the other. Since we're not going to be using calculus at this stage, we can say that elasticity is the percentage change in one variable per percentage change in another. Thus, the price elasticity of demand equals the percentage change in quantity demanded per percentage change in price, or

$$E = \frac{\%\ \Delta\ in\ Quantity}{\%\ \Delta\ in\ Price}$$

or

$$\frac{\dfrac{\Delta q}{q}}{\dfrac{\Delta p}{p}}$$

Actually, life would be a great deal simpler if we could use simple calculus in this case. We really want to talk about rates of change at a point on the demand function. If we talk in terms of percentages, then we lose the point change and get an average change in some segment of the demand curve. A look at Figure 3.11 shows you what I mean. If I want to find the elasticity of point *a*, then I have to find the average elasticity for the line segment around *a*. As you will see, just because the demand curve illustrated is a straight line, this does *not* mean that elasticity stays the same along the line. *Slope* and elasticity are *not* the same thing.

To find the average elasticity of the line segment around point *a*, we first must find the change in price. Price changed from $7 to $6 or $1. The average value of price over the range of the change is $6.50—halfway between the beginning price and the ending price. Therefore, the percentage change in price will equal $1/$6.50, or about 15 percent. Quantity changed from 1 unit to 2 units as the result of a 15 percent change in price. The actual change in quantity is 1 unit and the average value of quantity over the change was halfway between 1 and 2 units, or 1.5 units. The percentage change in quantity is therefore 1/1.5 or approximately 67 percent. In this range, then, a 15 percent change in price produced a 67 percent change in quantity demanded. To find the elasticity, we simply divide 67 percent by 15 percent and come up with the *coefficient of elasticity* of about 4.5. All that this figure tells us is that on the average within the range, a 1 percent change in the price of the good produced a 4.5 percent change in the quantity demanded. Since the coefficient of elasticity is greater than one, we say that demand in this range is *elastic*. A given percentage change in price produces a *larger* percentage change in quantity.

Now move down the demand curve toward the lower righthand end. Note, as price is decreasing, a given price change such as $1 gets to be a larger and larger *percentage* change. The Δp_2 is staying the same ($1) but the p_2 is smaller, therefore percentage change $(\Delta p_2/p_2)$ is getting smaller. At the same time *q* is getting larger so that any given Δq_2, such as 1 unit, becomes a smaller and smaller percentage change. As a result, the coefficient of elasticity must be decreasing, as indeed it is. In the price range between $2 and $1, the percentage change will equal $1/$1.50 or about 67 percent. At the same time, the percentage change in quantity is now 1/6.5 units or about 15 percent. The coefficient of elasticity equals 15 percent divided by 67 percent or approximately .22. In this range of the demand curve, a one percent change in price produces only a .22 percent change in quantity demanded. With the coefficient of elasticity of less than one, we say that demand is *inelastic* in that range. Were the elasticity coefficient

Figure 3.11
Comparative Price Elasticity

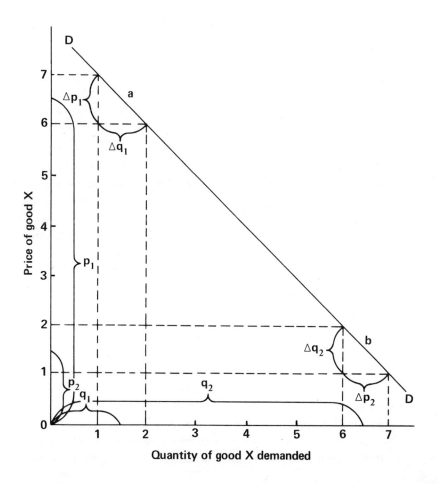

equal to one, it would mean that percentage changes in price produced exactly equal percentage changes in quantity demanded. The demand would have *unitary elasticity*.

There are many ways in which price elasticity of demand is used, but one of the more common applications is in measuring the impact of a change in price on the total revenue or total expenditures on some product. Let's construct the schedule of prices and quantities on which the demand curve in Figure 3.11 is based.

Price of X (in dollars)	Quantity Demanded	Total Dollars (Price × Quantity)
7	1	7
6	2	12 *E > 1*
5	3	15
4	4	16 *E = 1*
3	5	15
2	6	12 *E < 1*
1	7	7

Note, as price decreases, the quantity demanded increases, and at the high price end of the schedule quantity increases are sufficiently large so that total revenue actually *increases*. A price *decrease* results in a total revenue *increase*. It is no accident that this occurs in the elastic range of the demand schedule. The price elasticity of demand refers to percentage changes in quantity given percentage changes in price. Total revenue, or expenditure if you prefer, is the product of price times quantity.

$$TR = p \times q$$

Price and quantity are moving in opposite directions. As price goes up, quantity goes down, and as price goes down, quantity goes up. If a *percentage* change in one is offset by an equal and opposite change in the other factor, then *TR* (total revenue) won't change. This is the case when there is unitary elasticity. If a percentage change in price produces a *greater* percentage change in quantity demanded, then quantity demanded and total revenue will move in the same direction (quantity up, total revenue up; quantity down, total revenue down). For the other possibility, if a percentage change in price produces a *smaller* percentage change in quantity, then total revenue and price will move together (price increases, total revenue increases; price decreases, total revenue decreases). All we have done is describe the relationship between an elastic demand and total revenue, and an inelastic demand and total revenue. With an inelastic demand, price and total revenue move in the same directions. With an elastic demand, price and total revenue move in opposite directions.

There is an old chestnut of an example that makes a good lead-in to the next chapter on costs and levels of output. While the example itself may seem farfetched, the principles it illustrates are very useful. Assume for the moment that one day you're digging around in your backyard and your shovel hits something very hard. You give it an extra heavy belt and, lo and behold, out of the ground comes a stream of yellow liquid with the force of Old Faithful. No, you haven't hit the sewerage line, you have struck a *beer well*. Don't ask me how it got there. I haven't the foggiest idea. But there it is spewing the finest quality brew skyward with no cost to you or anyone else. When the word gets out, people come from miles around to see this strange freak of nature and carry off the stuff. They even bring their own containers and are careful not to trample the yard so here again, there is no cost to you in "marketing" the beer.

To make our example even more perfect, let's assume that you set out to get a monopoly position in your industry. You want to be the only seller in not only beer, but also all of the products that might possibly substitute for beer. First of all you get your friends in the National Guard to ring the city with troops and stop any and all competing products from entering the area. This would include not only beer, but whiskey, maybe pot, soft drinks, etc. Then you have your other friends in "the mob" break up and destroy any existing stocks of competing goods in the city itself. Now you're set to have your fun. Now you can charge just as much as you want for the beer, and no one will have any alternative but to pay, right? Not quite. People still have an alternative, and that is *not to buy*.

Well, this fact of life doesn't stop you for long. Since you studied a principles course in economics, you decide to carry out a little market research. You want to find out just what the demand in your marketing area is for your product. After studying reams of historical and cross-section data you find that the demand curve facing you as the one and only beer industry around looks like Figure 3.12. The question you must decide is what price you are going to charge for your product. Right off the bat, the demand curve lets you know that you can't charge just any

Figure 3.12
Elasticity and No-Cost Output

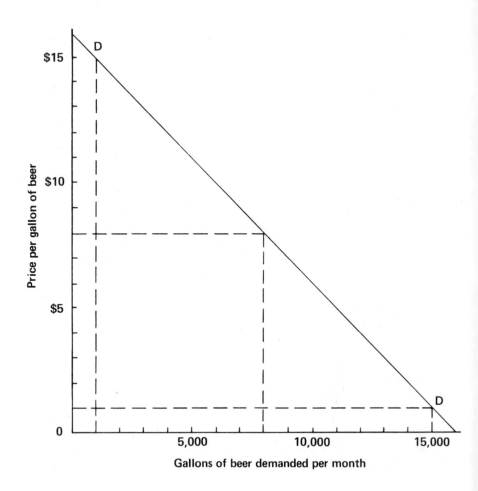

old price you want, because above $16 per gallon, nobody is going to buy it. If you charge $15 per gallon, you can sell 1,000 gallons, which isn't too bad. But can you do better? Well, if you lower price to $14 per gallon, you will double your sales. Remember extra sales are costing you nothing. It's all gravy, so the $14 per gallon times the 2,000 gallons is all profit. This $28,000 is better than the $15,000 at the $15 dollar price, so it will pay to lower the price to at least $14 per gallon. Try it again. At $13 per gallon, the quantity you will be able to sell rises to 3,000 gallons. This means $39,000 of revenue, again better than the revenue at the $14 price. If you kept doing this, pretty soon you would hit an $8 per gallon price which yields a revenue of $64,000 per month. If you lower the price still another dollar, sales will rise to 9,000 gallons, but total revenue in this case starts to drop and will continue to drop for further price decreases. You, as a monopolist will *not* charge the highest possible price for your product. You will charge the price which yields you the maximum net profit. In our simple example with zero costs, this means you will charge the price which maximizes your total revenue. With a straight line demand curve such as the one illustrated, this means you will lower your price to the point where the elastic portion becomes the inelastic portion. At that point elasticity is unitary and total revenue will be maximized.

Someone may ask why you don't sell the person that is willing and able to pay $15 per gallon his beer at the maximum price and then do the same thing for each price below the $16 figure. In other words, why don't you capture all of the consumer surplus by being what is known as a *discriminating monopolist*. Actually, this is a fine trick if you can pull it off. But pulling it off is not without its problems. Since we have assumed a free and unlimited supply of your product, let's say that you sell every potential customer for beer the quantity he is willing and able to purchase, right up to the 16,000 gallon quantity, at which no one is willing to make any further purchases at any positive price. Once this is done, you will probably find your neat little monopoly jeopardized by some chiselers. What is to prevent the person who purchased beer at $1 per gallon (because that was all it was worth to him) from selling his beer to people on the upper end of the demand curve who are willing to pay a great deal more. Of course, this is what will happen, and your $15 per gallon customer will tell you to go to blazes because he can get his cheaper from the chiseler. There will still develop a market price and it will be at $8 per gallon as before (assuming perfect information and perfect competition in this second mar-

Figure 3.13
Elastic and Inelastic Demand Curve

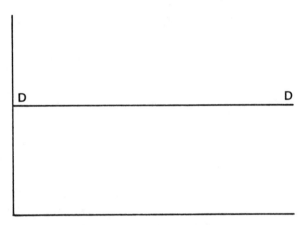

Quantity demanded per unit time
3.13a. Perfectly Elastic Demand.

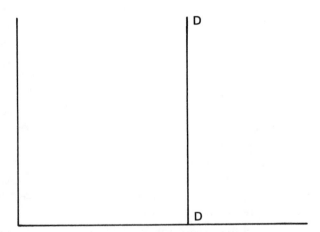

Quantity demanded per unit time
3.13b. Perfectly Inelastic Demand.

ket) but in this case you will receive only half as much as before. The beer you sold was to the people on the lower half of the demand curve. They in turn sold their beer to the people on the upper half of the demand curve. Now if you were strong enough, and could prohibit the kind of secondary sales just described, then you would be in the best of all possible worlds. There are few perfectly discriminating monopolists around, but when you find one, he will probably be doing very well indeed. As you will see in the next volume on micro-issues, the friendly heroin peddler may well be such an animal.

One more point should be mentioned in passing before going on to the subject of supply. A demand curve can be *perfectly elastic* or *perfectly inelastic*. These two special cases are shown in Figures 3.13a and 3.13b respectively. A perfectly elastic demand curve merely says that an infinite quantity will be demanded at the given price. At prices higher than the given price nothing will be demanded. At prices below the given price, an infinite amount will still be demanded. For the perfectly inelastic demand curve, the interpretation is that there is one quantity which will be demanded regardless of the market price. A change in the price will have no influence at all on the quantity demanded. Put another way, the quantity demanded is completely independent of the market price.

As mentioned before, the idea of elasticity has many applications. For example, if we discuss the percentage change in quantity demanded per percentage change in income, this is known as the *income elasticity of demand*. Inferior goods have negative income elasticities while superior or normal goods have positive income elasticities. As with price elasticity, income elasticity measures the *degree* of inferiority or superiority. When talking about related goods, the idea of *cross-elasticity* can be used to define and quantify substitute and complementary goods. Cross-elasticity refers to the percentage change in the *quantity demanded* of one good given a percentage change in the *price* of another good. If this elasticity is positive, then the two goods are substitutes. If the relationship is negative, the goods are complements.

Now that the subject of demand has been introduced, it is time to enter the world of costs—the world of supply. With a modest command of this tool combined with your "new" knowledge of demand, we will be prepared to look at the operation of the markets in the system.

Chapter Four   Supply

When we discussed the determinants of demand, there was a whole formula full of variables that influenced the quantity of a good people were willing and able to purchase. In one way, the answer to the question of why people are willing to supply a good or service is a bit simpler. It depends completely on the *cost* of doing so. Of course, there are several different kinds of costs involved, and that is the subject of this chapter.

To begin with, break these costs into the price of the good itself, the cost structure for the factors of production, the technology available, and the marketing costs facing the supplier. In symbols, we will say that

$$q_s = f(p, C, T, ICP_s)$$

where

q_s = quantity supplied.
p = the price of the good.
C = the cost structure for the factors of production.
T = the available technology.
ICP_s = the transactions costs facing suppliers.

At first thought, you may wonder why the price of the good itself represents a cost to the potential supplier. It's the same old story of opportunity cost. Perhaps an example of your own labor supply would best illustrate this. If you are supplying your labor for $2.50 per hour, this wage rate represents income but it also represents the cost to you of *not* working. It is the same thing for the potential supplier of any good. The market prices for the goods he *could produce* are a measure of the alternative uses of the productive factors under his control. The price of the good he is actually producing is a measure of his income, but it is also a measure of the resources he would forego were he *not* to produce the good in question. The higher the price of the product, the higher is the cost of not producing it. Therefore, in general, one would expect that increased product prices would tend to call forth increased production. One would expect that the normal supply curve—the schedule of prices and quantity supplied—would be upward sloping to the right as in Figure 4.1.

As was the case with demand, *supply* is defined as the relationship of product prices and the quantity people are willing and able to supply. Supply is *not* the same as *quantity supplied*. Again, as with demand, this relationship is described on a *ceteris paribus* basis. All the other factors affecting the willingness and ability of people to produce the good are held constant. In the case of demand, the relationship between price and quantity was always inverse. A change in price produced a change in the opposite direction in the quantity demanded. With supply, we *generally* assume that the price of a product and the quantity supplied will be a direct relationship. As the price of a good increases, so will quantity supplied. However, there are important exceptions to this generality.

The thing that everyone thinks about when the subject of making something comes up is the cost of what goes into the product. This is the variable that we are calling C in our supply function. It represents the whole structure of the costs involved in getting the necessary factors of

Figure 4.1
A Supply Curve

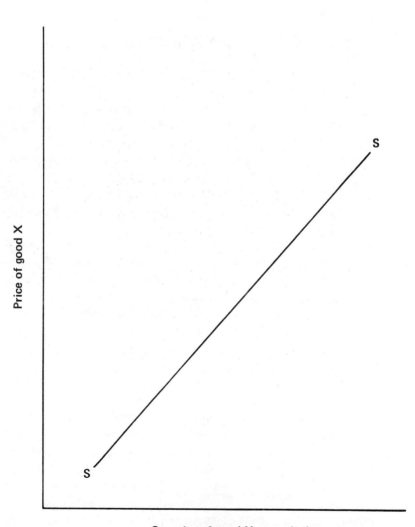

Quantity of good X per unit time

production to make the good concerned. Factors of production can be broken down many different ways but one of the more common groupings is as follows:

1. Labor
2. Entrepreneurship
3. Capital
4. Natural Resources

A few words describing each of these categories is in order before proceeding further.

Labor, as used by the economist, is much broader than the usual meaning of the word. As we will use it here, labor means any human effort resulting in the production of something that someone wants. This effort can be, and often is, very remote from the product itself. For example, the labor of the garage attendant who washes the company car of General Motors' president may seem very remote from the Chevrolet automobile in the showroom. But nevertheless, his labor was indirectly involved in the production of that Chevrolet. Similarly, the president of GM is probably not used to being considered "labor." But, to the extent that his services are productive, at least a portion of those services would be counted in the economist's definition of labor. Another part of those efforts might be counted in the next category, entrepreneurship, but for the most part, in a corporation the size of GM, Mr. President is just another input of administrative labor. So-called "professionals" often hate to be considered anything as low and common as labor, but for our purposes, they are. The physician, lawyer, teacher (God forbid), artist—all these again are part of the productive process and their human effort is classed as labor.

The second category, *entrepreneurship*, is really a special form of labor. It is, however, of such great importance to the productive system that it deserves special note. The entrepreneur is the guy who puts all the pieces together and comes up with a productive package. He does not necessarily invent something new, but he does constantly seek new ways to combine factors to obtain and maintain efficient production. For a small private firm, identifying the entrepreneur is usually quite simple. However, in the huge combines that exist today, this identification is considerably more difficult. Usually, the *entrepreneurial function* is diffused throughout the organization so that no one person could really be called *the* entrepreneur. Of course, this function exists even in completely planned economies, although I'm sure many would not like to admit it. Somewhere someone has to do the putting together and make the decisions involved in the allocation of factors.

The next general type of factor is called *capital*. Again, there is some problem because the word "capital" has some everyday meanings that are a bit different from those used by economists. Capital is anything that has required the use of scarce resources which in turn is used to produce something else. Therefore, a machine tool is a piece of capital. A factory building is also a piece of capital. A stock certificate *by itself* is not capital. It may represent partial ownership of some piece of capital. But by itself, it is not productive and does not qualify for the economic definition.

There is another kind of capital that many people overlook, which, in this country particularly, is a major portion of the country's productive stock. This type of capital consists of investments in *man*—human capital. The most obvious examples of this investment are found in the area of education and vocational training. But in addition, such items as health programs (public and private) also fall into an investment category. There are those that object to even talking about "investment" in human beings. They feel that this "depersonalizes" and demeans the human. The objection may have psychological merits, but treating such programs as education in any other way leads to some dangerous and erroneous conclusions.

Basically, resources in any community can be used up for immediate utility—they can be consumed or they can be used to increase future productivity by investing in the increase of productive capacity. In the latter case, the productive process uses up a portion of the capital with each unit produced or with the passage of time. We say the capital *depreciates*. The important difference between consumption and investment is the time period over which the good concerned yields services, and thus utility. Long-term use implies an investment, while short-term or immediate use usually suggests that the good is a consumption good. When resources are spent on education, there are several products that result. Some of these accrue to the individual while others are gained by the community at large.

To begin with, almost all education in this country has as *one* of its goals the increased future productivity of the student. This is certainly not to say that education is obtained just to make more money. But "making money" in a market economy is part of the game. Making money means that somebody or some group is willing to give up their resources to obtain something you are producing. Making money, figuratively, not literally (if you make it literally you may be in big trouble with the Feds), is the market's signal that you are doing something that other people want. To the extent that resources spent on education do improve productivity, then these resources are truly *invested*. By the definition of an investment, the term applies. Note, the investment will "pay off" for you by increasing your income. It will "pay off" for society by your increased ability to produce things society wants and for which it is willing to pay.

While we're on the subject, let's look at a couple more products that can come from the educational process. A portion of your education may be for *present consumption*. Some people actually enjoy going to college, for example. The social setting, perhaps the athletic events, and even the studies themselves may yield present utility to some students. To the extent that this is true, the resources spent on education are *not* an investment. In this case, the expenditures are just like those made on a good steak dinner or a bottle of whiskey. The gaining of present utility is the only goal and the only accomplishment. Another more common product of a "liberal" education can be another kind of investment. This investment is made to gain an improvement in the future "quality of life" of the student. Gaining the ability to understand and enjoy good literature would be an example. Gaining a better insight into the world around you *may* make your life more fruitful later on without necessarily increasing your ability to earn more money. Finally, in a free society, the ability of its citizens to understand and take part in their roles as citizens can well be the difference between the life and death of the society. Educational resources which help produce this result can also be viewed as a capital investment with potential returns to both the individual and society.

Obviously, most education will be a combination of the elements discussed above. For example, a student of English Literature may enjoy studying Shakespeare *right now*. He gains present utility from the learning process itself. In addition, he may gain the ability to enjoy reading Shakespeare at various times throughout the rest of his life. Here is investment for future personal consumption. Finally, he might be foolish enough to become a professor of English Literature. In this case, there would be an investment in future productivity as well.

Whether it be capital of a human or non-human type, the productivity of any modern economy depends heavily on the use of capital as one important input into the production processes. The basic facts of life about capital are these: First, it uses resources to create—it does not just come from nowhere. Second, to get it implies that consumption of some form is being deferred. Someone has to give up something now in the hope of future gains. Third, because it results in production and is scarce in the economic sense, the market can be expected to reward the holders of capital in proportion to the value of such productivity.

The final category of productive factors is really a special form of capital. We will call it *natural resources*. In the early part of the nineteenth century, economists were particularly interested in this factor of production. The reason for this interest was primarily the fear that first of all agricultural land, and later coal to fuel the industrial revolution, would run out leaving man both hungry and without industrial potential. Then technology came booming through with fantastic ways to maintain and increase the fertility of farm lands, and later with the development of alternative energy sources to supplement or replace king coal. The early part of the twentieth century saw a decline in the interest in natural resources. The general feeling was that whatever came up in absolute short supply would somehow be replaced by a technical miracle. As a general rule, this has actually happened, and as a matter of fact, the operation of the marketplace has even assisted the substitution process by raising the prices of inputs as they became relatively more scarce. This has provided the incentive for factor substitution and spurred the development of new resources.

But something else has been happening that has renewed the interest and concern for natural resource economics. Since the beginning of time, man has viewed certain things within his world as limitless, costless, and therefore free. Primarily, this attitude has existed towards flowing air and flowing water. Sure, the occasional stream got wrecked by a papermill, but there were a thousand others that stayed clean. So the industrial area of a city had air that was almost deadly. You only had to stay there during working hours and then you could go uptown where the dirt was only a memory. For quite a while, this was no particular problem. Given the level of the population, the level of industrial production, and the price of waste products, pollution was an occasional nuisance, but never something of international concern.

Several things have happened recently with geometric rapidity. Population levels and rates of increase have snowballed. Simultaneously, productivity has risen so that consumer goods are being produced and consumed at record levels—*more people* are all consuming *more goods*. This kind of arithmetic is bound to cause problems, but in addition, because of our wealth and productivity, the cost of recycling waste products has gone up. There was a time not too long ago when people made livings collecting old rags, scrap metal, old bottles, etc. True, it was a lousy living, but given the alternative employments, it was as good as any available for many people. Subsistence living like this is now pretty much confined to those who literally cannot work and for some quirk in imperfect laws cannot get a subsistence living from welfare programs. Maybe this is a better way to organize the economy, but one should not be surprised to see the collection and recycling of junk deteriorate when the relative return to such activity falls dramatically.

It is very difficult to define a "natural resource." All resources have some natural components to them. But generally we consider natural resources as those having fixed quantities and incapable of being regenerated or replaced once used. Coal would certainly be one of these, as would any of the so-called fossil fuels. But air and water can be depleted, too, if used or misused in certain ways. A papermill operating in the wilds of northern Canada may pollute the air with particulate matter, stench, and other gaseous components. However, moving air in nature has the built-in capability of cleansing itself from certain pollutants given time, space, and tolerable levels of initial polluting. It's entirely possible that the polluted air will be as pure as the driven snow (and I don't mean snow in Chicago) by the time it hits any population centers.

On the other hand, the same pollutants per ton of output dumped into the air in Gary, Indiana will overload the natural waste disposal capacity of the air by many times. Now there is a problem; air is being used as though it were a free good. The waste disposal capacity of air and water are *not* free goods. At least they are not free when other people begin to have costs imposed on them because someone else is using the air and water for crud disposal.

In the analysis that follows, we will treat all factors as being either capital or labor. In the volume of this series covering microeconomic issues, we will again look at some of the differences of factors within these two broad groups. Pollution will be one of the specific issues covered as will be the impact of different groups within the labor category.

Costs, then, are generated because firms have to pay factors of production for their efforts. Some of these costs will affect the output decisions of the firm and some of them will not. Since this whole chapter is discussing quantity supplied, the difference between these two types of costs deserves mentioning. First, in the long run a firm or an industry can vary all of the factors which it uses to produce a good. In fact, this is precisely how we define "the long run" as far as production is concerned. The actual length of time that the long run represents will be different for different firms and different industries. But again, by definition the long run for any firm or group of firms is the length of time necessary to vary all of the inputs and outputs with which the firm is involved. Any time period shorter than that we call the "short run."

Again, by definition, the short run for any firm implies that there is some factor or group of factors that the firm cannot vary. It is stuck with something used in the productive process and cannot vary its use of the *cost* of its use. In the short run, it is a *fixed factor*, and from fixed factors come *fixed costs*. All we mean by a fixed cost is that if the firm is to stay in business, there will be certain costs involved with or without production taking place. In other words, there will be costs that, once incurred, will not vary as the output of the firm varies. I'm sure you can think of examples of this sort of thing. If a company buys a factory building, it will have to pay interest on the money it borrowed to buy the building, or lose the interest it could have earned had its own money been used to finance the purchase. In addition, the ravages of time are bound to cause some expense whether anything is produced in the building or not. There will be maintenance expenses and depreciation costs as well. These may not vary either, whether or not the company produces one unit in the factory. Sometimes these costs are called "sunk costs." Once they are made, you've had it. Only if you sell the building or go out of business can you vary that type of cost. Remember now, this is in the short run. In the long run you *can* vary this kind of cost by selling, buying a new building, going broke, or running off to South America with the company funds.

In Figure 4.2 the relationship between fixed costs and output is shown graphically. Two kinds of fixed costs are illustrated. The true fixed cost is shown by the line labeled *FC*. You will note that as output rises, nothing happens to the level of this cost; it stays the same. The line labeled *FVC* shows a different but equally interesting situation in which costs stay constant over a range of production and then jump up to another level for another range, etc., etc. This is the sort of thing one would expect if a new

Figure 4.2
Fixed Costs

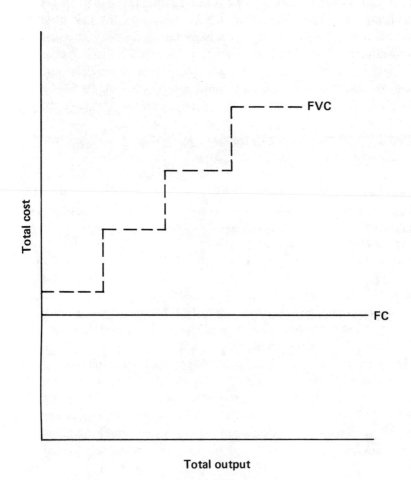

**Figure 4.3
Constant Costs**

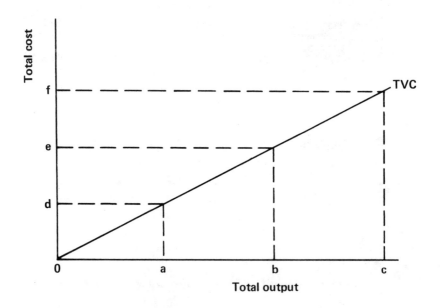

building were required every time production got to a certain point. This type of cost is fixed over ranges and then jumps up "step-wise" when production increases; it is both a fixed and a variable cost.

The other kind of cost is so-called *variable cost*. As the name implies costs in this category vary with output. As output is increased, so are the costs. As output is decreased, so are the costs. If there are 200 pounds of steel in a refrigerator, then for each refrigerator the manufacturer turns out, 200 pounds of steel will be added to his cost. If he produces 10 units, his steel cost will be 2,000 pounds. If he produces 2,000 units, his steel cost will amount to 400,000 pounds. This is not only a variable cost, but also a variable cost that is directly proportional to output.

If all costs of a firm were directly proportional to output, we would say that the firm was operating with *constant costs*. Note, constant in this case refers to the fact that the *rate of change* in costs is constant as output varies. Total costs will *always* increase with the increase in the production of an economic good. This is definitional since the production of an economic good means that scarce resources are used to make it. Were this not the case, the good would be free.

Figure 4.3 illustrates a case of constant variable cost. In this case, the firm has no fixed costs, so at zero production there are zero costs. From that point on, every increase in production brings forth a proportionally equal increase in costs. The total cost line is straight and through the origin. Equal increases in output require equal increases in costs; $Oa = ab = bc$, and the costs to get these equal increments are $Od = de = ef$. The notation *TVC* obviously stands for *Total Variable Cost*. We will be using this notation for a while, so it would be a good idea to memorize and get used to it.

Variable costs do not always increase proportionally. In some cases, costs do not go up as fast as output. Proportionally, there is a decrease in the additional costs with additions to output. This happens often when plants that are built for some particular capacity are then operated at levels of output much below this capacity. The variable factors are not producing as efficiently as would be the case at higher output levels. In this circumstance when output is increased, the old factors, as well as new ones added, work more efficiently. Therefore, total cost is not increased in proportion to the increase in output. Figure 4.4 illustrates this type of TVC.

One type of industry where this *decreasing cost* takes place is in the

Figure 4.4
Decreasing Costs

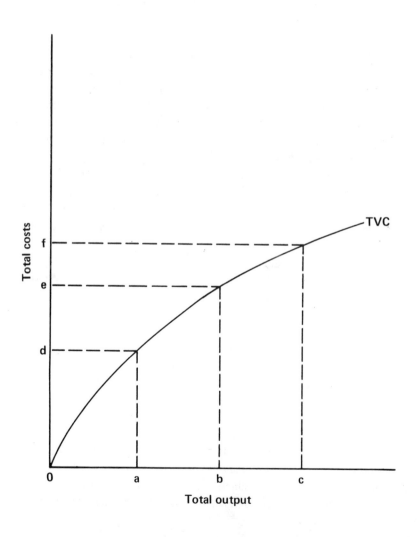

generation of hydroelectric power. Here both the physics and economics of the operation are such that within very broad limits, the larger the generating plant, the less it will cost to produce *additional* units. *Please remember*, total cost is increasing in all of the examples we are using. But it is the *way* total costs increase that determines whether there are *constant* costs, *decreasing* costs, or as in the next category, *increasing* costs.

Looking again at Figure 4.4, *Oa, ab*, and *bc* are again equal increments of increased output. But in this case, the increase in costs associated with successively greater outputs gets smaller. *Od* is greater than *de* which, in turn, is greater than *ef*.

Almost every type of productive operation going runs into a cost curve that looks like Figure 4.5 at some level of production. A firm can duplicate existing plants or build bigger, more efficient plants, but sooner or later proportional costs are bound to rise. Of course, the scale at which this happens may be very large, but again, there is bound to develop some cost-increasing problem. It may be nothing more than the ability of management to handle large scale, or it may, and often is, the sheer bureaucracy that seems to be a corollary to large size. Anyway, this increasing cost situation merely means that equal increases in output can be successively obtained only by larger proportional increases in costs. In the illustration, *Oa* can be produced for *Od* of cost; *ab (=Oa)* can be produced only for a larger chunk of costs, *de*. Similarly, *bc (=Oa = ab)* can only be produced for a larger cost increase, *ef*.

Most firms actually operate with a cost curve that looks more or less like the one in Figure 4.6. In the short run, there are usually fixed costs over which the firm has no control once they are made and assuming the firm stays in business. This is shown as line *FC* at an initial cost level of *Oc*. At low levels of production, the firm experiences decreasing costs. Over production range *Oa* costs increase proportionally less than production. Then there is normally a range of fairly constant costs such as output between *a* and *b*. Finally, costs start rising as in the graph beyond point *b*.

Practically all of the analysis requiring a study of costs could actually be handled by using only the concepts just developed. However, a further breakdown of cost structures can be of assistance in understanding their application and importance. In the next few paragraphs we will be talking about *average costs* and *marginal costs* and their relationship to both the total cost picture and production decisions that go into the idea of supply.

Average cost is very simple. If I want to find the average of any two

Figure 4.5
Increasing Costs

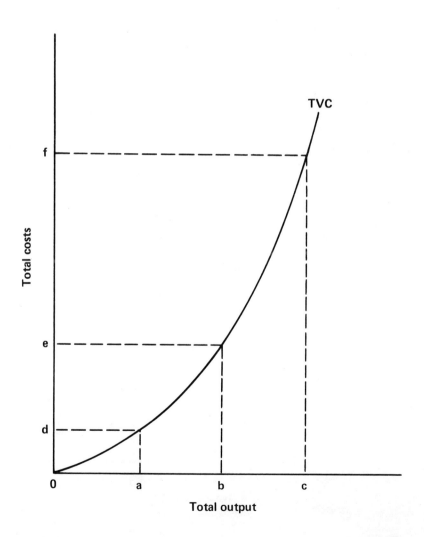

Figure 4.6
Total Costs

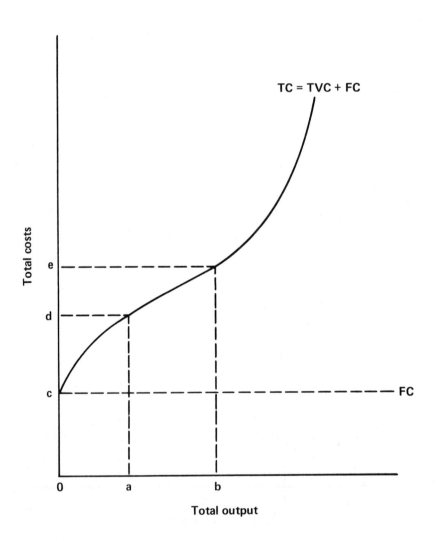

related variables, I just divide one of them by the other. If I buy 10 oranges for $1.50, then the average cost of each orange is $1.50/10 or $.15 each. On the other hand, if I want to know the average number of oranges I can get for a dollar, the division becomes 10/$1.50 or 6.7 oranges *per* dollar. To find the average cost of any given level of production, all that has to be done is to take the total cost at that point and divide it by the total production. This gives the average number of dollars being spent to produce one unit of the product. If I want to find average total cost (*ATC*), then total cost is divided by total output. If I want to find average variable cost (*AVC*), then total variable cost is divided by total production. In Figure 4.7, the derivation of average costs is shown graphically. As you will see shortly, we are much more interested in variable costs than fixed costs, so in the illustration, fixed costs have been assumed away. If you wish, you can consider this a long run cost curve. Remember, in the long run all costs become variable.

Taking a series of points on the total variable costs line, construct straight lines through the origin of the graph. You can easily see that the slope of these lines will be the ratio of the vertical axis (total costs) to the horizontal axis (total output) at that point on the function. Starting in the decreasing cost portion of the function, as we construct additional lines through the origin, their slope decreases; average cost is decreasing. Even in the constant cost range of the curve, average cost continues to decrease. The slope of *b* is less than *a*. The slope of *c* is less than *b*, and the slope of *d* is less than *c*. Note particularly the average line *d*. This one is just tangent to the total cost curve, and from that point on out, additional average lines, such as *e*, will begin to have increased slope. At the tangency point, average cost is at a minimum.

The lower part of Figure 4.7 merely plots the changing slopes of the average cost lines. In the range from *a* to *d*, average cost is falling while beyond *d*, the average cost rises. Point *d* is the minimum. Note, in this graph the vertical axis is merely labeled "dollars." We are going to be putting some different functions on this same graph in both the cost and revenue departments, so the general value of "dollars" will be used from now on.

The concept that probably blows more minds of beginning economics students than any other is the whole idea of *marginal* changes. It has already been introduced in the idea of the marginal rate of substitution and now it is time to talk about *marginal costs*. The marginal costs are

Figure 4.7
Derivation of Average Cost

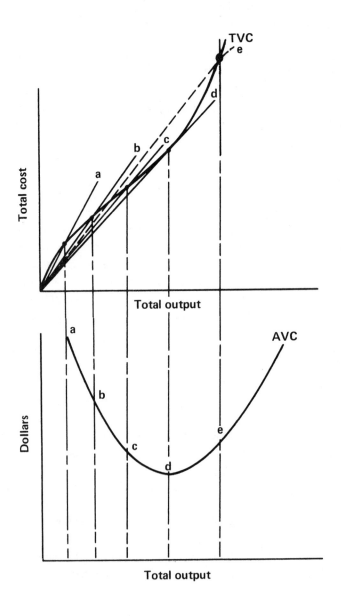

those which are associated with the production of an additional unit of output. To be exact, it is the *rate* at which costs are changing with changing output. What kind of costs affect marginal cost? Will fixed costs influence it in any way? The answer to this last question is obviously no. Fixed costs are just that—*fixed*. They do not change with output. Therefore, fixed costs will not have anything to do with marginal costs. How about variable costs? The answer here is that marginal cost is precisely the rate of change in variable costs. Marginal cost measures which direction and to what degree the variable costs of a firm are changing with changes in output.

As usual, a look at the graphs is in order. Figure 4.8 shows a decreasing cost segment of the total variable cost curve. To produce the first unit of output, the cost is *0a*. For the first unit, the total variable cost is *0a*, the average variable cost of the first unit is *0a*, and the marginal cost of the first unit is *0a*. Now we come to producing the second unit. The second unit will cause an *additional* cost of *ab*. The marginal cost of the second unit is *ab*. The total variable cost of producing both units is *0b*. The average cost of producing the two units is *0b/2* or the slope of line *c*. It is fairly easy to see intuitively that the rate of change in total costs will be represented by the *slope* of the total cost curve at the given point. The important difference between this slope and the slope of the average cost line is that the average cost line always goes through the origin while the slope of the cost function is just the slope of a tangent line on the curve. With this information, let's see what's happening in terms of totals, averages, and marginals. At the one unit output level, the slope of the total cost curve is represented by line *d*. At the two unit output level, the slope of the total cost curve has decreased as represented by line *e*. In other words, marginal cost, the rate of change in total cost, has decreased. Note also that the slope of the average cost line, *c*, is steeper than the slope of the marginal cost line at the same point. In other words, the marginal cost is less than average cost. In this range of decreasing proportional costs, the *additions* to total cost will be less than the *average* cost of all previously produced units. Again, this is easy to see; if I have been paying an average price of $.15 each for oranges, and then I am able to buy one for $.10, then the new average is going to be less than the previous. When the marginal cost of something is less than the previous average cost, average cost will be falling. In the range of decreasing costs, then, marginal costs will be below average costs. Average costs will be falling, but do not forget,

Figure 4.8
Marginal Costs and Average Costs

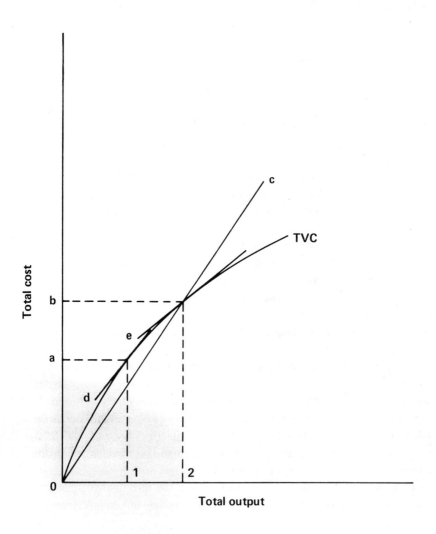

total costs are still on the increase with increased output. The only thing is that they are increasing at a decreasing rate.

Now consider the situation when increasing costs are the pattern for the firm. Figure 4.9 illustrates this possibility. The cost of producing the first unit equals *Oa*. The cost of the second unit is *ab*. In this case, the cost of the second is greater than the cost of the first. The slope of line segment *e* is less than the slope of segment *f*. Note also that for both the 1 and 2 unit points, the slope of the marginal cost line is greater than the slope of the corresponding average cost line. Marginal cost is greater than average cost, and therefore, average cost is increasing; in fact, it is increasing. Average cost line *d* is steeper than average cost line *c*.

Now let's put the whole mess together and see if it has really been worth all the effort. In Figure 4.10, the now-familiar S-shaped total cost curve is drawn in the upper graph. In the lower panel, the corresponding average and marginal curves are presented. In the area of decreasing costs, the total cost curve bends upward away from the horizontal axis. In this area, marginal cost is actually falling. This is precisely what we mean by decreasing costs. The costs of producing additional units is less than the cost of producing previous output. Marginal cost is also below average cost. (In this case, we will assume long run, and therefore no fixed costs.) From the range of decreasing costs, output proceeds into the range of constant costs. In this range, marginal cost remains constant. The cost of producing additional units stays the same, and the *MC* curve is horizontal for this short segment. Note, however, that marginal cost is still below average cost at this juncture. This means that average cost will continue to decline, but at a slower rate than before.

Before the minimum point of average variable cost is reached, the firm encounters the range of increasing costs. The cost of producing additional units begins to rise. As marginal cost rises, average cost falls even more slowly, until finally the rising marginal function and the falling average function are of equal value. At this point, the amount added to total cost is exactly the same as the previous average cost, and for that instant, average cost does not change. Beyond that point additions to cost *exceed* the previous average figure. Marginal cost is above average cost, and therefore, average cost begins to climb. Given the S-shaped total cost curve, average cost will always decline, reach a minimum, and then climb. Marginal cost will always be below average cost to the left of the minimum point, equal the average cost at the minimum point, and be greater than average cost to the right of the minimum point.

Figure 4.9
Marginal Costs with Increasing Total Costs

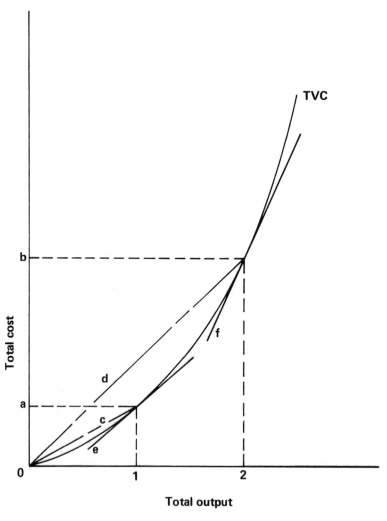

Figure 4.9 Marginal Costs with Increasing Total Costs.

Figure 4.10
Total, Average, and Marginal Costs

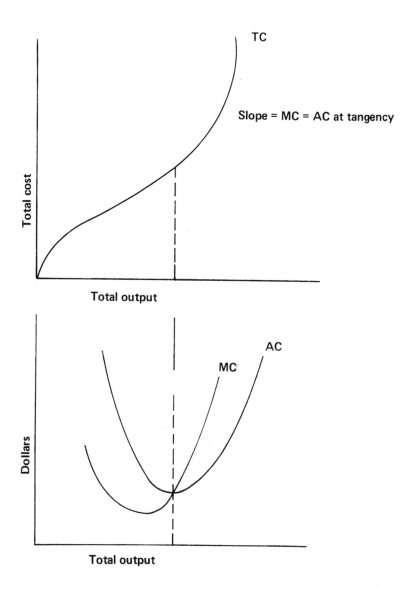

Figure 4.10 Total, Average, and Marginal Costs.

Finally, we are ready to talk about the actual decision a firm will make regarding the level of output they will produce. This discussion will cover the situation for a competitive firm. The ramifications of the discussion for a pure monopoly are presented in the next volume on microeconomic issues.

We will start with the assumption that firms wish to maximize something called *profit*. Profit for the economist is a bit different from the profit usually calculated by the accountant. The formula for profit looks the same.

$$\pi = TR - TC$$

where

π = profit
TR = total revenue
TC = total cost

Total cost in our case actually includes some items that most accountants would call "profit." It includes the minimum return necessary to keep factors producing the quantity of output under discussion. For labor, it means that wages are high enough to prevent laborers leaving the firm or industry, but not so high as to entice other laborers into the field. This really is not very different from the accountant's handling of labor costs. But the same criteria for minimum returns also apply to the holders of the capital in the firm and to the entrepreneur as well. The economist counts as a cost the opportunity costs of the factors. The minimum return to holders of capital required for them to leave their capital in the firm is handled as a cost by the economist. The minimum return required by the entrepreneur(s) to keep the entrepreneurial function going is also counted as part of TC. Therefore, when the economist speaks of *profit*, he is referring to a gain of resources to the firm in excess of the minimum required for the firm to produce any specified level of output. Sometimes this item is called *economic rent* instead of profit.

Anyway, the firm is assumed to try and maximize this kind of profit. It is not interested in charging the highest price for its product. It is not interested in just making costs as low as possible and revenues as high as possible. It is interested in making the *difference* between total revenue and total costs as large as possible.

If an industry is competitive in a pure and theoretically perfect sense, there are several characteristics that must hold. First of all, the firm is a *price taker*. The individual firm has no influence over the price of the good in the marketplace. Individually, they are faced by "the" market price for their product which will go up and down according to changes in supply and demand. But whether the individual firm lives or dies, whether it triples its output or stops producing altogether, the firm's production decisions will not, by *themselves*, have enough impact to substantially alter the market price of the product.

Graphically, this situation can be shown by making the demand curve for the product of the individual firm perfectly elastic. This then says exactly what was described above; the firm can produce and sell as much or as little product as it wishes without experiencing a change in the price of its product. Of course, the price may change for other reasons which would then be shown as an upward or downward shift in the perfectly elastic function. Figure 4.11 illustrates the point. At price *Ob*, the firm views its demand curve as *DD*. It can sell as much or as little as it wishes without affecting price. If something happens in the market to raise the price of good X, then the demand curve as viewed by the firm will rise to *D'D'*. Now the price for the firm's product is *Oc* for any and all quantities. In a similar manner, a decrease in demand would shift the perfectly elastic demand curve down to some lower price such as *Oa*.

This demand curve facing the firm has some very special interpretations because of its perfectly elastic nature. First of all, it represents *the* market price. It is the price the firm will receive for any or all of its output. The market price is the same as the *average revenue* that the firm receives for its product. Since it is receiving the same price for all its output, the average revenue and price must be identical. But since average revenue is not changing, then the amount added to total revenue by selling one more unit must be the same as average revenue. *Marginal revenue* must also be constant and equal to average revenue, which is indeed the case. The demand curve facing an individual firm in a perfectly competitive industry is equal to the average revenue curve of the firm, the price schedule faced by the firm, and the marginal revenue received by the firm.

Demand $= p = AR = MR$

There is one confusion to be avoided. While the demand curves for each firm in a competitive industry are perfectly elastic, this in no way implies that the demand curve for the total product of the industry is also per-

Figure 4.11
The Demand for a Good to a Firm in Perfect Competition

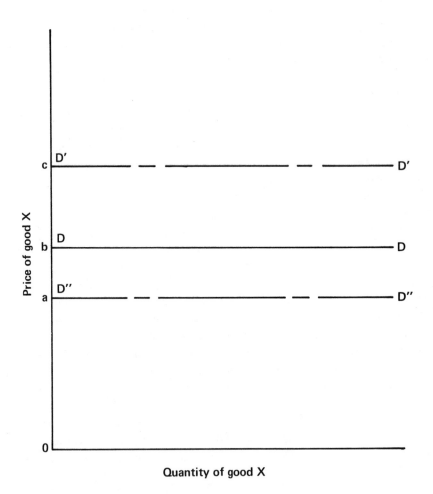

fectly elastic. In fact, it may be very inelastic as is the case for certain farm products produced and sold under competitive conditions, but having a total industry demand that is highly inelastic.

Finally, it's time to put the bits and pieces together and see what they're all about. In Figure 4.12 a demand curve is plotted along with the cost curve of the firm. Now let's look at some points of possible production. First, no firm can operate for long if the average cost of production exceeds the average revenue received for its product. This produces losses, and the firm will go out of business. Therefore, the firm cannot operate at any point to the left of output *Oa* nor to the right of output *Ok*. In the range between *a* and *k*, however, the average revenue is at least as large as average cost so that potential profit exists. One might think that output *Ob* would be a good choice. At this level, the *average profit* is the greatest. The difference between average revenue and average cost is the greatest. Average cost is *Od* and average revenue is *Of*. Average profit is therefore *df* per unit of output. But the firm is not interested in average profit, but rather *total profit*. To find total profit, the length *df* is multiplied by the output *Ob* to obtain the area *dfig*. This is *not* the largest "profit box" that can be obtained. To prove this we go to the all-important marginal functions.

At output *Ob*, the revenue the firm could get by producing and selling one more unit equals *Of*, the marginal revenue for all outputs. The cost of producing one more unit is equal to *Od*. In other words, the firm can take in more than it pays out if it raises its output. It can *add* to total profit. As long as this is the case, the firm will continue to expand output until the point *Oc* is reached. At this point the cost of producing one more unit exactly equals the revenue received from one more unit. Further production would reduce profit rather than increase it. Beyond this level of output the marginal cost would exceed marginal revenue and total profit would be cut.

Here you have the development of the foremost axiom of choice for a firm: A firm will produce at that level which will maximize profit. Profit will be maximized at that output where revenue received from the last unit equals the cost of producing that last unit. Below this level, total profits can be increased by increasing output. Above this point total profits can be increased by cutting output.

In Figure 4.12 our firm is making an economic profit. Remember, "normal" or minimum profit is already included in the cost curve. When

Figure 4.12
A Competitive Firm with Short Run Profits

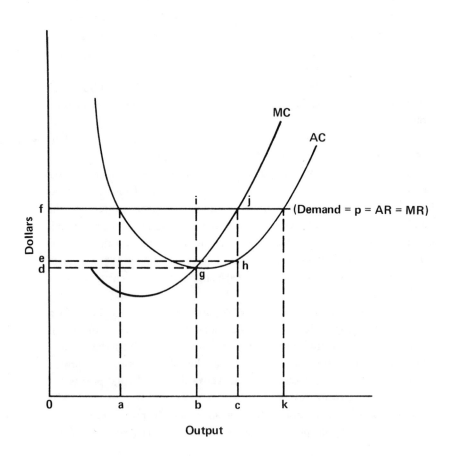

our cost and revenues are equal, the firm is still making sufficient profit to keep it in business. The profit per unit is represented by *ef* and total profit is represented by the box *efjh*. But we are talking about a firm in a competitive industry. If this kind of profit exists for the firm and other people find out about it, then others will get into the act and output for the industry will increase. Remember, *for the industry* the demand for the product is not completely elastic. As a result, entry into the industry by new firms will raise industry output. The increased output can be sold *only* at a lower price. The price in the market will fall lowering the demand for each firm including the newcomers in the industry.

The lower price cuts the excess profit until finally, $TR = TC$. There is only enough return to each and every factor of production to keep them from moving to their next best alternative. All economic rent or excess profit has been squeezed out by the falling price. Figure 4.13 shows this equilibrium situation. Demand for the firm has fallen from D to D' because of the increased production within the industry. For the firm here, this has caused a reduction in its output to Ob. The price it receives is Od, and this point is on the minimum of the average cost curve. At this equilibrium point, average revenue, average cost, marginal cost, and the price of the product will all be the same.

Whether you realize it or not, we now have the supply curve developed for the individual firm in a competitive industry. This supply curve is nothing more than the marginal cost curve of the firm. Since the competitive firm must take the market price as given, there is nothing he can do about the marginal revenue part of the production decision. The marginal cost curve, however, shows all of the points at which he would be willing to operate were the price of the product at the several levels. There's one qualifier to this statement; if the average revenue he receives is below the average variable costs at that point, he will not continue to operate. Therefore, the supply curve of the firm is that portion of the *MC* curve *above* average variable cost. Note, fixed costs have nothing to do with the production decisions of the firm. They are sunk costs and will not change with production changes. In the long run, *all* costs become variable so that a *short run* fixed cost will influence *long run* production decisions.

The next step is simple. To find the supply curve of a competitive industry, we add up all of the supply curves of the firms within the industry. This gives a "first approximation" of the actual industry curve since it assumes that increased use of factors by the industry will not raise

Figure 4.13
A Competitive Firm in Long Run Equilbrium

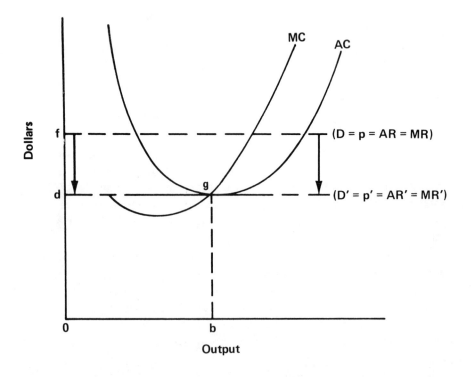

Figure 4.14
Deriving the Industry Supply Curve

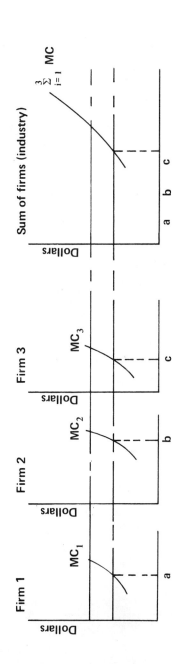

the wages paid to the factors. There is no problem with this assumption if the industry does not represent a major employer of any of the factors. But in the event that increased output by the industry *would* raise the wages to any or all of the productive factors, the supply curve would be steeper than the sum of the marginal costs curve shown in Figure 4.14.

Changes in the other two arguments of our supply function, technology and transactions costs, merely shift the marginal cost curves of the individual firms. Increases in any of these costs shift the marginal cost curves back to the left, and decreases in costs shift the curves to the right. Increased costs decrease supply, and decreased costs increase supply.

Chapter Five

Free Market Operation

Most of the practical discussion of market operation will be carried out in the next volume of this series on microeconomic issues. However, a few moments should be spent here showing the interaction of the supply and demand functions developed in this book. Reviewing our demand function, remember that

$$q_d = f(p, p_c, p_s, i, t, ICP_d)$$

and

$$q_s = f(p, C, T, ICP_s)$$

Figure 5.1
Supply and Demand in the Market

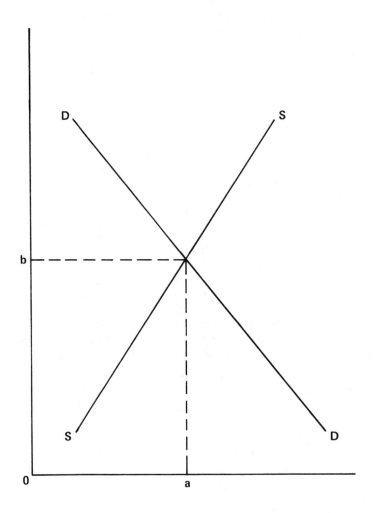

Figure 5.2
Price Too Low in the Market

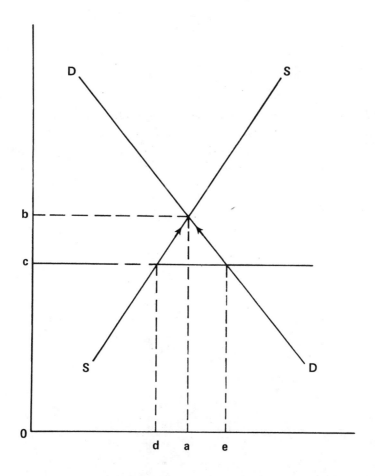

Figure 5.3
Price Too High in the Market

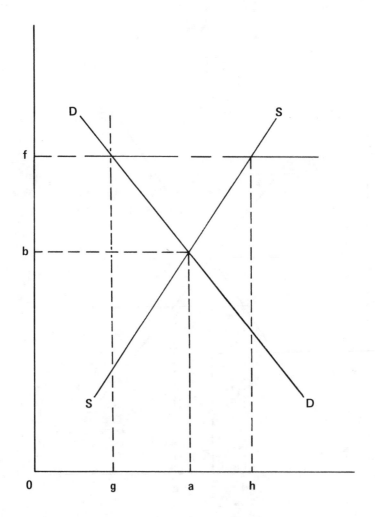

Note the arguments in each function are unrelated to any other argument in the other function, *except* the price of the good itself. Remember, too, that demand is an inverse relationship between price and quantity, while supply is generally a direct relationship between price and quantity.

In Figure 5.1 this combination is graphed. The supply curve *SS* slopes upward to the right, while the demand curve slopes downward to the right. At one point, the two functions have the same value of both price and quantity, price *Ob* and quantity *Oa*. At this point equilibrium is said to exist. There are no forces tending to change either price, quantity supplied, or quantity demanded.

To demonstrate this equilibrium, let's see what happens if, for some reason, the price strays from the equilibrium. First, in Figure 5.2 a price below equilibrium "happens" at *Oc*. At price *Oc*, the quantity people are willing and able to purchase rises from *Oa* to *Oe*. But at the same time, the quantity people are willing and able to supply falls from *Oa* to *Od*. The quantity demanded exceeds the quantity supplied and an *economic shortage* exists. As a result, demanders of the product will start to bid against each other for the limited quantity, thus bidding up the price of the good. As the price begins to rise, the demanders are willing and able to purchase less, and, at the same time, the suppliers are willing and able to produce more. Both of these movements help reduce the shortage until finally the original equilibrium position is restored at price *Ob* and quantity *Oa*.

In Figure 5.3, the opposite situation is described. If for some reason the price of the good moves to *Of* (greater than *Ob*), then the quantity supplied will rise to *Oh* while the quantity demanded will fall to *Og*. We have now developed an economic surplus with more stuff around than people are willing and able to purchase. In this case, competition between the sellers will bid down the price as the excess goods are being disposed. As the price falls, quantity supplied also falls, helping to reduce the surplus. At the same time, quantity demanded rises at the lower prices. Again, this continues until the equilibrium position is reached once more.

There you have it, the market operation in a pure world of perfect markets and competition. The primary purpose of the whole exposition has been to provide some simple tools of analysis that can be used to assist in the understanding of real-world problems. Those problems are the subject of the next volume covering microeconomic issues.